ADD Children:
A Handbook for Parents

ADD Children:
A Handbook for Parents

To Order Call:
1-630-859-6752

The ADD Clinic
Dreyer Medical Clinic – Advocate Health Care

ADD Children:

A Handbook for Parents

John N. Blair, M.D.
Director, ADD Clinic
Dreyer Medical Clinic – Advocate Health Care

JB Enterprises
Aurora, Illinois

© 1999 by John N. Blair M.D.
All rights reserved.

Cover design by Bobette Wolf
Illustrations by Sean Connell

Printed in the United States of America

JB Enterprises

For more information, contact:
Dreyer ADD Clinic
1870 W. Galena
Aurora, Illinois 60506

Publisher's Cataloging in Publication

(Prepared by Quality Books Inc.)

Blair, John N., M.D., 1945-

      ADD children: a handbook for parents/John N. Blair M.D..

p. cm.

ISBN 0-9674306-0-7

1. Attention-deficit hyperactivity disorder 2. Parenting. 3. Medical.
I Title

Dedication

This book is dedicated to helping ADD children and their families cope with the problems of Attention Deficit Disorder (ADD). It is not meant to be all encompassing but intended more as a quick guide. I have tried to put together the best ideas on how to handle the problems associated with ADD. These ideas have come from working with thousands of ADD children over the twenty-five years of my clinical practice.

I would also like to thank my ADD daughter who has been both a joy and frustration to be around. She has been an inspiration to me and provided me with many stories and anecdotes about living with an ADD child. Although she has not always appreciated my sharing some of her exploits, she has been tolerant of her father. To see her grow into a capable young woman, who has learned to compensate for her handicap and become successful, has made the frustrations of dealing with ADD bearable. She has helped me help other parents deal with their ADD children.

Acknowledgements

This book would not have been possible without the support and help of the staff of the ADD Program at Dreyer Medical Clinic – Advocate Health Care: Marlene Erdman - Social Worker, Linda Green - Educational Diagnostician, Linda Hardie - Audiologist, Roger Hatcher - Pediatric Psychologist, Tom Waller - Computer Specialist, Cindy Zamorski - Nurse and Program Coordinator and Sharon Kochik - Nurse and Program Director.

Special thanks to Nancy Hopp, Ric Calabrese and Anne McKearn for reviewing the manuscript and their encouragement.

I would like to acknowledge two other individuals. The first is Morris Green, M.D., who was the Head of Pediatrics at Indiana University during my medical school and residency training. He instilled in me the belief that the psychosocial aspects of disease are often more important and challenging than the medical aspects. The second person is Mel Levine, M. D., who was Director of Behavioral Pediatrics at Harvard during my mini-fellowship. He provided me and all pediatricians with a framework for helping ADD and LD students.

Table of Contents

Overview ix

Successful Parents xi

1. ADHD and ADD Without Hyperactivity 1
2. Labeling 13
3. Causes and Theory 19
4. Prevention 29
5. Recruiting the Team 35
6. "TEACH" and the Win-Win Approach 43
7. Behavioral Problems 59
8. Dealing with the Adolescent 79
9. School —— What the Parent Needs to Know 83
10. Behavioral and Educational Strategies —— School ... 95
11. Associated Problems and Their Treatment 111
12. Medication 117
13. Controversial and Alternative Therapies 145
14. Adult ADD and Outcomes 149

Selected References 154

Overview

In writing this book, I have discovered several truths about raising ADD children:

1. ADD is a handicap. A handicap is something that interferes with being successful. ADD is not a handicap that can be seen, but it can be as damaging and painful as any physical handicap. It certainly affects not only the child but also siblings and parents.

2. The old African proverb that it takes a village to raise a child is especially true with ADD children. He or she requires four times the parental energy of an average child. No one person has all the answers. A team composed of family, friends and professionals are needed to help guide and mold the child.

3. ADD children are affected both by their wiring (medical) and their environment (classroom and home). Medication can help the ADD child's wiring problem but is not a cure-all. It does not help the child's environment. Finding accommodations and modifying the

ADD child's environment can be more effective than medication in helping the ADD child find success in life.

4. "Practice makes perfect." ADD children have problems with paying attention, getting things done in a timely fashion, social skills, etc. They must work on improving these weaknesses in order to be successful.

5. Motivation is the key to success. ADD children tend to avoid working on anything that requires sustained attention. They need to be more motivated than other children.

6. All children need positive self-esteem in order to be successful. ADD children find it difficult to have positive self-esteems because the nature of their handicap causes people to criticize them for being impulsive, hyperactive and inattentive. The parent must set up situations in which the ADD child can be successful. Success breeds success. Failures should be regarded as lessons towards success rather than all negative.

7. Parents need to learn how to find win-win solutions for problem areas. They must find positives even when things seem overwhelmingly negative. This truth will be discussed in more detail in the chapters on behavioral management.

8. Medication is not a cure all. Medication can lead to dramatic improvement in behavior, but it does not insure success. The most effective treatment of ADD children consists of educational, behavioral and psychological support along with the judicious use of medication when needed. See the chapter on medication.

9. Parents must keep a sense of humor. The only way to deal with adversity is with a smile on your face. Many of the ADD child's antics are humorous when viewed retrospectively. Wearing a smile when the child is use to frowns can make management much easier! See the chapters on behavior.

10. ADD Children can be successful. Most ADD children turn into successful adults. They learn to use their creativity and energy in productive ways. The parent's job is to guide them along a path toward success.

Successful Parents

All parents want their children to become successful in life and to reach their potential. As outlined above, this is no small task for parents of ADD Children. Parents of successful children do two things well. They teach their children to *make good choices* and they teach *the value education.*

ADD children have choices to make (argue with parents or not, do homework or not, etc.). The key to teaching children to make good choices is to limit the number of options available and to make bad choices more painful than good choices. The parent changes the arguing choice from (arguing or not) to (don't argue and get praised or argue and get to do a chore). Children soon learn that it is in their best interest to control their impulses to argue. See the chapter on "TEACH" and the Win-Win Approach.

School is one of the most painful places for the ADD Child. In school the child is asked to sit still, pay attention and do written work. These tasks are very difficult for the ADD child. It is important to build an educational foundation for the ADD child. The parents need to spend time with their children on educational activities on a daily basis. This should start with reading to the child in infancy and continue with a daily homework activity starting in kindergarten. This says to the child that the parents think school is important. It also prevents a struggle over getting homework done in future years. See the chapters on school.

1

ADHD and ADD Without Hyperactivity

Symptoms

Mrs. Brown has a child named John who is in first grade. He can't sit still and he is constantly on the go. He can't keep his hands to himself and he is failing several subjects. He bothers the teacher and his classmates. John is frequently sent to the principal's office and mom is always getting calls from the school.

Mrs. Brown has tried everything in an attempt to control John's impulsive and hyperactive behavior. Nothing has worked! Not time-out, not scolding, not spanking. John has also been seen at the emergency room several times for injuries from falls. Mrs. Brown felt sure that she was going to be reported for child abuse. She even admitted that she feels like spanking him when he is at his worst.

John fits the classification of a child with Attention-Deficit/ Hyperactive Disorder (ADHD). These children have problems with paying attention, being distracted, being hyperactive, and being impulsive. The symptoms must be present before the child is 7 years of age and have lasted for at least 6 months. The symptoms must cause significant social, academic or occupational problems.

This is a handicapping condition that requires parents to become expert in parenting, psychology, motivation, education, and medicine. The parent of an ADD child cannot afford to be average but must become a five star coach with lots of energy. The parent must stay several steps ahead of the child in order to guide the child in the right direction. Otherwise, the child wanders aimlessly. This is not an easy task even for the best of parents!

Classification

- ADHD combined type with both inattention and hyperactivity impulsivity
- ADHD predominantly inattentive type
- ADHD predominantly hyperactive-impulsive type.

The children need to meet six of the criteria under inattention to be classified as inattentive and six of the criteria under hyperactive-impulsive to meet that criteria. The old terminology is ADD with hyperactivity and ADD without hyperactivity. Because all the above classifications have many things in common, the term ADD will be used throughout the book to represent all the above classifications unless otherwise specified.

**Diagnostic Criteria for Attention Deficit Hyperactivity Disorder*

A. Either (1) or (2):

1) six (or more) of the following symptoms of **inattention** have persisted for at least 6 months to a degree that is maladaptive and inconsistent with developmental level:

   Inattention

   a) often fails to give close attention to details or makes careless mistakes in schoolwork, work, or other activities
   b) often has difficulty sustaining attention in tasks or play activities
   c) often does not seem to listen when spoken to directly
   d) often does not follow through on instructions and fails to finish schoolwork, chores, or duties in the workplace (not due to oppositional behavior or failure to understand instructions)
   e) often has difficulty organizing tasks and activities

f) often avoids, dislikes, or is reluctant to engage in tasks that require sustained mental effort (such as schoolwork or homework)
g) often loses things necessary for tasks or activities (e.g., toys, school assignments, pencils, books or tools)
h) is often easily distracted by extraneous stimuli
i) is often forgetful in daily activities

2) six (or more) of the following symptoms of **hyperactivity-impulsivity** have persisted for at least 6 months to a degree that is maladaptive and inconsistent with the developmental level:

Hyperactivity
a) often fidgets with hands or feet or squirms in seat
b) often leaves seat in classroom or in other situations in which remaining seated is expected
c) often runs about or climbs excessively in situations in which it is inappropriate (in adolescents or adults, may be limited to subjective feelings of restlessness)
d) often has difficulty playing or engaging in leisure activities quietly
e) is often "on the go" or often acts as if "driven by a motor"
f) often talks excessively

Impulsivity
g) Often blurts out answers before questions have been completed
h) Often has difficulty awaiting turn
i) Often interrupts or intrudes on others (e.g., butts into conversations or games)

B. Some hyperactive-impulsive or inattentive symptoms that cause impairment were present before age 7 years.
C. Some impairment from the symptoms is present in two or more settings (e.g., at school [or work] and at home).
D. There must be clear evidence of clinically significant impairment in social, academic or occupational functioning.

E. The symptoms do not occur exclusively during the course of a Pervasive Developmental Disorder, Schizophrenia, or other Psychotic Disorder and are not better accounted for by another mental disorder (e.g., Mood Disorder, Anxiety Disorder, Dissociative Disorder, or a Personality disorder).

*Reprinted with permission from the *Diagnostic And Statistical Manual Of Mental Disorders, Fourth Edition.* Copyright 1994 American Psychiatric Association.

All children have some of the above characteristics. Some children have most of the above characteristics, but they are only present a small percentage of the time. We find the same characteristics in normal children, but normal children have fewer of the characteristics and they are less predominant and they do not interfere with the child's social, behavioral and educational functioning.

If a child has some of the characteristics above and if those characteristics interfere with success academically, behaviorally or socially, the child has a problem that needs to be dealt with. It makes little difference whether you label the child as ADD or not.

ADD is a handicap that makes life more difficult. It doesn't mean that ADD children or adults can't pay attention, but that it is harder for them to pay attention to what others want them to focus on. Some ADD children can focus on Nintendo or Lego's for hours. However, they can't focus on the schoolwork for longer than a minute. They must be more motivated than other people or they lose their attention and their work is not completed.

Terminology

The term **ADD** will be used throughout this book to represent all children who fit into one of the above classifications. When important the subdivision will be specified.

Diagnosis

Mrs. Smith said that she could tell that Bill was going to be an active child because he was constantly moving in utero. When he was born he continued to be active and colicky. She felt like she wasn't a very good parent because she could never get Bill to calm down. Her friends had babies who would calm down easily. As Bill became a toddler, Mrs. Smith became depressed because of Bill's behavior. She couldn't even hold him because he was so active and he would end up kicking her or hitting her. She found it hard to like her son and she felt guilty for having these feelings.

Not only does Bill have the precursors of ADD but his behavior has caused further problems with the mother-child relationship. It is our feeling that children with ADD experience social, psychological, and educational problems because of their handicap. Their families also experience many problems and frustrations because of difficulties that ADD children cause. Therefore, it is important not to evaluate a child for ADD problems in isolation but to also evaluate whole child and the child's role in the family.

Determining whether a child has ADD or ADHD varies from easy to difficult. A very active child with impulsivity is easy to diagnose because this stands out from the other children. However, a girl with only attention problems and distractibility is difficult to spot in a classroom with twenty-eight other children. The following things should always be done to be certain of the diagnosis:

- History
- Hyperactivity and Attention Rating Scales
- Hearing and Vision Screen
- Physical and Neurological Exam
- Auditory Processing or Visual Processing

Depending on the presenting problems the following should be considered:

- Learning Disability Tests
- Laboratory Tests

History

Problem Areas

The history is obtained by getting reports from the parents, school, and the child if over age 8. The history should contain information on the mother's pregnancy, the child's birth, and medical history. Most clinics give the parents and the older child questionnaires to fill out. The teacher is asked to fill out a current progress report on the child. The school is asked to send a report on any educational testing that has been done. Old report cards are also helpful in determining where the problems are. These are then reviewed with the family at the time of a clinic visit. Once all this information is accumulated it is easy to get a picture of the child's strengths and weaknesses.

Strengths

In addition to looking at problem areas, it is important to determine what interests and talents the child has. ADD is a handicap that makes life harder for the child. School tends to bring out the worst in the child. He or she is asked to sit down, be quiet and get work done in a timely fashion. All of these things are hard for the ADD child to do and frustration with the school situation can result. The child then drops out or acts up. If the parents can find areas in which the child is successful, they can help build self-esteem and hopefully motivate the child to work hard on the school areas that are more difficult.

Hearing and Vision

The child should have a hearing and vision screen. We still find a few children each year who appear to have ADD but really have a hearing problem.

Physical

A physical with a review of the medical history should be done to make sure there are no underlying medical conditions aggravating or causing the attention or hyperactivity problems or both. It is important to focus on difficulties during the pregnancy and delivery that might have caused neurological problems. It should be determined whether there are any diseases that run in the family or whether the child has any chronic medical problems that might interfere with the ability to concentrate. The clinician needs to know if the child is using any medications on a regular basis. Certain medications can cause either attention or hyperactivity type of problems. It is also important to inquire about any sleep difficulties because lack of sleep can aggravate both attention and hyperactivity problems.

Objective Testing

Many clinics are measuring the child's ability to focus on visual and auditory stimuli. They are using standardized testing that compares normal to ADD children.

Auditory Processing

Auditory processing tests require the child to listen to a stereo tape through stereo headphones and repeat what was heard. The tapes can put noise in one or both ears making it difficult for the child to attend to the important information. The scores on several tests can determine if the child has problems processing auditory information when a distraction is present. If the child has problems with these tests, it is suggestive that he or she has problems with attention.

Visual Processing

Visual processing tests are also used. The Gordon test is a computerized visual test that rates children on visual distractibility, impulsivity and vigilance. The Continuous Performance Test and the Matching Familiar Figure tests also check visual attention but are less comprehensive than the Gordon. These tests can help determine if the child is visually inattentive or impulsive.

Laboratory Tests

Routine laboratory testing of blood is not routinely done unless there are some indications of a medical problem from the history or the medical-neurological exam. EEGs (brain wave tests) are a waste of money unless there is a history of seizures, staring spells or bizarre changes in a child's behavior.

Learning Disability Testing

If the child is having significant problems in school with academic areas, learning disability tests should be done. These consist of tests that measure the child's academic achievement and tests that measure the child's potential or IQ. Some experts recommend that all children who might have ADD should have these tests, but we feel that is not necessary if the child's major problem is attention and not academic failure.

Making the Diagnosis

Once all the information is gathered and analyzed, a diagnosis can be made. Actually we prefer to describe the child's strengths and weaknesses rather than make a diagnosis. However, insurance companies, schools and parents want a diagnosis. If the child has attention and or hyperactivity problems as defined under DSM IV (see the criteria presented early in this chapter) and these problems are interfering with success socially, academically or behaviorally, then we make a diagnosis of ADD. We also feel it is important to formulate a treatment plan that includes any other diagnoses the child has and identifies the strengths and weaknesses of the child and family. By doing the above, the child has a better chance of being successful in the game called "Life."

ADD Without Hyperactivity

Mary is a twelve-year-old girl who has been experiencing school difficulties since third grade. She is failing in most of her classes. Her teachers say that she is not motivated and that she doesn't try to do her work. The school and parents have tried to motivate her with rewards, and they have used assignment sheets, and punishments. Nothing has worked and both Mary and her parents are very frustrated. Mary has become very difficult at home, refusing to do any schoolwork.

Mary's parents describe her as a pleasant child who is very kind and considerate of others. She is very enjoyable to be around. She perceives the world differently than other children. She takes great joy in observations that other children take for granted, such as "the hands on the clock move." She has lots of friends.

The only problems she has at home are getting organized to do chores and getting her homework done. It takes her one hour to do the dishes while it takes her brother twenty minutes. She has trouble getting up in the morning and getting everything done before she is to leave for school. Her room is a disaster area and it is impossible for her to find things in it. Mary has recently said that she is dumb and no good. She says that she has tried to do her homework and schoolwork but that "I just can't do it." She's angry with her parents and school because they keep picking on her.

The school has done a full educational evaluation on Mary. Her testing has shown that she has above average intelligence and that her achievement scores are grade appropriate in all subjects except grammar. Classroom observation by the psychologist noted that she was off task a majority of the time. She was not disruptive in the class and certainly had no signs of hyperactivity. She tended to fiddle with her hair barrettes and other objects in her desk. She seemed to have a hard time getting started on any assignment that required paper and pen.

Mary is a good example of a child with ADD without hyperactivity. ADD without hyperactivity is more common in girls with a 4 to 1 ratio of girls to boys. Many of these children are overlooked in the younger grades because they do not disrupt the class and they tend to be pleasant children who try to cooperate with their teachers and parents. They get into trouble when the amount of schoolwork increases and they are asked to concentrate more and produce more work. When they cannot perform up to the expectations of their parents and the school, they are labeled as underachievers or nonmotivated children. Many times they become depressed because they have problems getting work done even when they try. After awhile, some of these children stop trying and either act out or drop out.

Checklist

- Pleasant
- Girl
- Disorganized – room and school desk are a disaster area
- Takes forever to do homework or chores
- Sometimes called "air head" by friends

Problem Areas

Attention

The ability to sustain focused attention should increase as a child becomes older. ADD children without hyperactivity have just as much trouble focusing attention as do hyperactive children. Even when they try to focus on a task, they have difficulty.

Distractibility

Because these children have a free flow of thought, they are easily distracted by things that impinge on their senses. They will attempt to start a project and then become distracted by their own thoughts or some minor disturbance in their surroundings. Some of these children are labeled by their friends as "air heads, space cadets, or nits (not in today)."

Organization

Because of the above-mentioned problems, these children lack organization. They have not learned how to get themselves or their possessions organized. Most people learn organizational skills by trial and error or observation. Since these children do not process their observations, they do not modify or correct inefficient ways of accomplishing work. Many of them have to be taught even simple organizational skills.

Output failure

Children who are easily distracted and have organizational problems are going to have problems accomplishing tasks at home and in school. Many ADD children without hyperactivity also have minor learning disabilities or have missed whole areas in their education because of not paying attention. The combination of these problem leads to problems with producing written work.

As children progress through school, they are expected to do more and more written work that is dependent upon a mastery of the basic skills (handwriting, punctuation, spelling, etc.). Add to these skills the ability to organize a report, analyze information and it is easy to see why ADD without hyperactivity children have a difficult time with output of work. They often fail when asked to do written tasks. There is nothing worse for the parent-child relationship than sitting at a table trying to get a child to write a report and getting nothing done in one hour filled with frustration.

Easy child

These children are often described as easy children when younger because they were easy to manage as infants and preschoolers. In this case, their distractibility was an asset. If as an infant the child was fussy, the parent could easily provide a distraction and the infant would calm down. As a toddler, the child could be entertained with simple things like boxes and kitchen utensils.

Overly talkative

For some unknown reason, many of these children have a tendency to talk all the time. They are constantly interrupting adults to point out their observations. Many times their conversations are as unorganized as their written work and this can drive their parents or teachers over the edge.

Daydreamers

This is a problem that can be easily missed by the school and the parents because the child can look attentive. Unless you observe the child very closely or ask a specific question, you would never know that the child is not paying attention.

Treatment Guidelines

Teacher

- Help with organization
- Be aware of problem and give extra time
- See specific recommendations in educational chapters

Parents

- Tutor for study skills and weak areas

- Work on organizational skills
- Use motivation strategies
- See specifics in educational chapters
- Raise self-esteem - find areas of expertise
- Provide counseling for depression if needed
- See chapters on behavior management

Medication

- Stimulant medication is very effective
- See medication chapter

Measurement Of Treatment

It is difficult to measure improvement in a nonhyperactive child. The only measurable improvement would be an improvement in grades and a decrease in the amount of time it takes to accomplish homework or chores.

2

Labeling

Labels

Children like John, the hyperactive boy, have real problems. Whether you want to label them as behavioral problems, motivational problems, or ADD makes little difference. The important thing is to try to figure out how best to help the child reach his or her potential. It would be great if we could do away with labels and look only at the child's strength and weaknesses. However, labels seem to be a necessary evil in today's increasingly complicated world.

What Are the Risks of Having a Child Labeled?

There are multiple risks in being labeled ADD in the school setting. The child could be given the wrong label and consequently get the wrong services. If the child overcomes the handicap, there is a worry that the label can't be changed and that the child would not be placed in regular education but be kept in the special education programs. Many parents worry that labels can become a self-fulfilling prophecy. The teachers expect the ADD-labeled child to be hyper, inattentive and a behavior problem and the child fulfills this expectation. Some health insurance companies have refused to insure families with ADD children. Most branches of the military require ADD recruits to be off all medications for a year.

While there are many concerns about being labeled, there are also benefits. Schools get funding from the government because of labels given to children with special needs. Without labels there would be no funds available for special programs. People use labels to help categorize problems. This allows professionals to try certain interventions for each category and then evaluate whether they work or not. Without labels we would spend a great deal of time describing the child and less time would be available for helping the child. Labels help us find strategies that have been proven to help children.

In general, labels are helpful for ADD students. Many schools are beginning to realize that ADD children can be successful if given a little extra help. These schools are beginning to instruct teachers in techniques that are helpful in focusing the ADD child's attention. Such techniques are also helpful for non-ADD children. They include allowing ADD children more time to complete their work and finish tests by letting them do work after school or over the noon hour. College entrance exams can now be taken in an untimed format. These accommodations for the ADD child have come about because of the use of labels.

Whether we like it or not the ADD child is probably already labeled. Many ADD children feel that they are stupid or bad. Their classmates often label them as "hyper" or "wild." Teachers have unofficially labeled the child as a "pain." Before deciding on whether a child should be officially labeled by the school, the parents should look at the benefits and the risks of labeling their child.

The major risk of having a child labeled is that it will become a self-fulfilling prophesy as noted above. Parents also worry about their children being kept in special classes and that the school will not work to get the child out of special education classes into the mainstream. The key to this problem is the teacher. Good teachers want children to reach their potential and will work hard at helping them attain success. Keeping kids in special education or having an inclusion aid is no longer much of a problem; schools lack funding and want kids in the regular class because it is cheaper.

ADD is a handicapping condition. Like children who have physical impairments, ADD children have impairments that interfere with their ability to function. This does not mean that the child cannot focus attention, learn or control behavior. What it does mean is that these tasks are more difficult because of the handicap. It takes ADD children more time and practice to become successful academically, socially and behaviorally. Used appropriately and carefully, labels can help the child to become successful, especially in school.

Other Labels – What ADD Is Not

There are groups of children that demonstrate some of the same symptoms that ADD children do but who could be classified as having a different diagnosis. ADD is not the primary problem if the child has one the following problems:

- Mental Retardation
- Psychiatric Disorders
- Neurological Problems
- Tourette's Syndrome
- Genetic Disorders
- Drug Toxicities
- Chaotic Families

Mental Retardation

Children with mental retardation and borderline intelligence have trouble with concentration. They have an inability to process information rapidly and to understand abstract thoughts. Usually educational and psychological testing reveal that they have low aptitudes for learning in all areas. Treatment for these children involves special education so they can learn at their own rate. Stimulant medication has been shown to improve concentration and performance in normal children and mentally retarded children. The benefits of stimulant medication are not as dramatic in retarded children as in ADD children.

Psychiatric Disorders

Autistic Children or Pervasive Developmental Disorders (PDD)

Children with Pervasive Developmental Disorders or Autistic behavior have problems with social interaction and communication and a restricted repertoire of activity and interests. They can appear oppositional and hyperactive especially when placed under stress because of their emotional lability. These children are identified by their unusual mannerisms which include poor eye contact, echolalia (repeating over and over again something they have heard), repeated self-stimulating activities, ritualistic behaviors, and delayed speech.

Autistic children need a comprehensive management program involving many professionals. Stimulant medication is occasionally of benefit for autistic children with hyperactivity or severe problems with attention. Occasionally, the stimulant medication increases bizarre behavior.

Asperger's Disorder

This is a disorder that is getting a lot of attention in the mental health community. Children with this disorder have some of the characteristics of autism and some of the characteristics of ADD. Their primary problem is impaired social ability: They tend to have poor eye contact, don't develop peer relationships, and don't share enjoyment, interests, or achievements with others. They have repetitive and stereotypical patterns of behavior, interests, and activities (hand flapping, rituals, etc.). There is no delay in speech or cognitive ability. In clinical experience these children have problems with attention in group situations even though attention problems are not listed in the criteria for Asperger's syndrome.

Mood Disorders

Children who use to be classified as Manic-Depressive are now classified as Bipolar under Mood Disorders in DSM IV. The difference between the Bipolar child and the ADD child is that the bipolar child is oblivious to the problems of his or her behavior. These children present as euphoric children who are inattentive to their environment and become fixated on certain ideas. This is comparable to the manic part of the adult manic-depressive. Frequently, the child has a parent or relative who has been diagnosed as having a Bipolar Disorder. All children who present with ADD symptoms who have parents with Bipolar Disorders should be evaluated carefully for a Mood Disorder. The treatment for this group of children is still in the investigative stage because it has only been identified recently. Lithium, a medication used with adults who have Manic-Depressive episodes, has been found to be effective with some children.

Depression is another diagnosis under Mood Disorders in the DSM IV. Depressed children have a hard time concentrating and are often confused with ADD children. Depressed children have low energy levels, appetite problems, and sleep problems. They also commonly have suicidal ideation and they feel dysphoric (down in the dumps).

Many ADD children become depressed by their chronic lack of success. It is important to figure out what symptoms are caused by the ADD and what symptoms are caused by depression. The treatments for the two conditions are different. If depression is the primary problem it should be treated before trying to treat the ADD problems.

Neurological Problems

There are degenerative neurological disorders involving the white matter of the brain which cause loss of intellectual function. At times children with these disorders can appear hyperactive or inattentive. These children deteriorate over time with the loss of intellectual abilities. ADD children do not have this progressive loss of intellectual abilities. There is no treatment for this type of disorder.

Petite mal seizures in children can be misinterpreted as attention problems. These children have staring spells of 3-8 seconds in duration, during which they do not hear or comprehend what is going on. An EEG (brain wave test) is diagnostic of this disorder. ADD children do hear what is going on and if they are specifically questioned can tell what just happened. Petite mal seizures can be precipitated by having the child hyperventilated (breathing deeply and rapidly). Treatment consists of anticonvulsant medication.

Wilson's Disease is a degenerative brain disease characterized by speech problems (dysarthria), problems with balance (ataxia), and mental changes (inability to focus attention). It is caused by increased levels of copper in the blood and is treatable with medication to remove the copper from the blood.

Tourette's Syndrome

Tourette's Syndrome (TS) is an inherited disorder that causes serious problems. The syndrome appears in childhood. Often there is an inability to focus attention. Over a period of years, the attention problems worsen and children develop tics such as uncontrollable jerking of the face and shoulder. This is followed by verbal tics where the children utter unusual sounds, such as grunts, barks or swearing. This disorder can become incapacitating. It causes social isolation and often the children are persecuted by their peers. Treatment consists of ignoring the tics if they are mild or a trial of behavior modification if the tics are bothersome. If the tics are incapacitating, medications are used. For a while, stimulant medication was not used to help the attention problems of these children for fear of precipitating severe tics. Recent research shows that about 50% of the TS children who have attention problems can benefit from stimulant medication without making their tics significantly worse. Stimulant medication is now tried carefully in children who have tics and significant attention problems.

Genetic Disorders

There are many genetic disorders that are associated with school problems and distractibility. Two of the more common disorders are Turners Syndrome and Neurofibromatosis. Turners Syndrome affects girls and is caused by a loss of one of the X chromosomes. The affected girls tend to be short in stature, have webbed necks, and have problems with attention. Neurofibromatosis can be recognized in children who have five or more brown pigmented spots on their skin the color of coffee with cream (cafe au lait spots). These children can have tumors in their brain that cause an inability to focus attention.

Drug Toxicity

As mentioned above many drugs can affect the attention center. If a child is on any chronic medication and has ADD, the affect of that medication should be considered in any treatment plan.

Chaotic Families

There are some families that do not function well. There is no order to their lives and no rules or guidelines for their children's behavior. The children in these families can appear to have ADD and hyperactivity. However, once order is restored to the child through help to the family or foster care placement, the symptoms soon diminish.

Summary

There are problems that can look like ADD or have some of the same symptoms. Many of the conditions noted can be helped by using the same treatments as are used for ADD children. However, it is imperative to treat the underlying condition first. Hopefully, by looking at the conditions that mimic some of the ADD symptoms, we will come to better understand the ADD child.

3
Causes and Theory

Mrs. Jones went to a school conference to discuss her son John. She was told that John was having both academic and behavioral problems. John was noted to be disruptive in the classroom and to not turn in his homework assignments. The school suggested some modification for the classroom. They also asked Mrs. Jones to set better behavioral limits at home and to make sure that John did his homework. Mrs. Jones was angry because she had already been trying to do both for over one year. She had asked for the school conference six months before it was scheduled.

Whose fault is ADD? Is it the school's fault for not giving the child enough individual guidance and attention? Is it the parent's fault for not establishing the correct path? Or is it biological? This chapter will look at theories concerning the causes of ADD.

Early Theories

Lack of Nurturing

The first theories suggested that ADD is a problem with nurturing. Parents are to blame for causing the child's bad behavior and associated problems because of faulty parenting. In other words, the parents, because of their own psychological difficulties, taught the child to be hyperactive and inattentive. This theory believes that ADD is learned.

In spite of the fact that we no longer believe this to be the case, this notion is still widely held in society. Parents may find it when they attend the child's school conference and the teacher suggests that the parents need to set better limits at home or when a relative suggests that the parents need to be more consistent. Intentionally or not, the implication is that the parent has not done their job correctly. Many parents become defensive when confronted with these attitudes. They waste time trying to defend their parenting skills instead of working with the professionals to find solutions for their children's ADD problems.

In summary, ADD is really nobody's fault. It is not the child's fault and it is not the parents' fault. It is the result of a biological imbalance in the child's nervous system.

Many parents who hear this for the first time are surprised and find it difficult to believe. Often they have developed their own theories as to what they did that caused the hyperactive behavior. They may think that Dad's drinking too much caused the ADD, or Mom's not setting enough limits caused the ADD, or marital problems generated the disorder. While it is true that these things maybe harmful, it is not true that they caused the ADD.

MBD

One of the older theories about what caused ADD was the minimal brain damage theory (MBD). It was felt that there had been some insult to the brain that caused actual physical or tissue damage which in turn caused the ADD symptoms to appear. This theory developed in part from the valid observations that children who had experienced encephalitis (a viral infection of the brain) sometimes developed symptoms of hyperactivity. Brain damage may cause hyperactive-like behavior in some children, but in general ADD is not caused by physical damage to the brain. The latest research suggests that ADD is a biochemical deficiency which affects the central nervous system (CNS) of the ADD child. Forty percent of the time this deficiency is inherited and ADD symptoms are seen in close relatives of the ADD child.

Recent Theories

The Brain

We have learned more about the brain and its development in the last Ten years than in all of recorded history. We have learned that the brain is like a sponge. It craves and soaks up information. It uses the outside world to shape itself. We have also found that there are crucial periods of time when the brain needs to be stimulated or it will not develop to its potential.

**Development of the wiring*sponge

The brain is a three-pound mass that goes through four stages of development. The first stage takes place during the first few months of gestation. The brain develops approximately 200 billion cells over these months. The cells of the brain need to be stimulated and are designed to get in touch with the senses.

In the second stage (20th week of gestation), one half of all the brain's cells die. These are the cells that did not get connected. During this period the brain becomes organized into forty different specialized areas (e.g. vision, language, motor areas). These areas are influenced by electrochemical stimulation. For example, male sex hormone tends to stimulate the spatial and math areas of the brain while female hormone stimulates the language centers. This might explain some of the thinking differences between men and women. This is a time when maternal ingestion of drugs can cause damage to the brain or change which cells are stimulated. Alcohol consumption by mothers during this time is felt to be the leading cause of mental retardation in the US affecting 1 in 500 children.

The third stage of development is roughly from birth to twelve years of age. This is the time when the brain becomes a super sponge for absorbing information. The connections between cells are multiplying exponentially as learning takes place. By four years of age, the basic architecture is established. The brain is very adaptable until age twelve. After that age, the child can learn new things like foreign languages but it takes more effort.

The final stage is the adult stage. By puberty one half of all the connections that were made have disappeared. This is why the brain is less adaptable. Potential different paths that weren't stimulated have disappeared and new courses are harder to pursue. By this time the brain has established 500 trillion connections between nerves. These connections can be changed but it takes more effort than when we had more connections waiting to be stimulated. Animal studies have shown that you can increase by 25% the number of connections by placing the animal in an enriched environment versus an environment void of stimulation.

*From Kotulak, Ronald (1993, April 11-15).

The Brain and ADD

Research by Dr. Alan Zametkin from the National Institute of Mental Health showed that adult ADD patients have an abnormality in the way that their brains work. In his study, Dr. Zametkin measured brain activity using PET scans of the brains of 25 ADD adults and 50 non-ADD adults. He found that the adult ADD patients had two areas in their brains that were less active than normal adults. These were the premotor cortex, which helps control motor movements, and the superior prefrontal cortex which is used when people pay attention.

This study suggests that ADD children's brains are "wired" differently than those of other children. Their brains seem to function in a different manner. They often notice things and remember things that others have missed or forgotten. This different way of perceiving and processing information is felt to be the result of an under active attention center.

How the Brain Works

The brain works much like a computer. There are specialized areas that deal with what is seen and heard. There are other areas that allow storage of information and areas that allow the use of information to create new ideas. There are still different areas that allow energies to be focused on one task at a time (the attention centers). These areas filter out nonrelevent material.

Imagine trying to watch TV, talk on the phone, and answer your children's questions while the stereo is blaring. Which stimulus is the most important and which stimuli are blocked out? Most people can respond to one stimulus and ignore the others. ADD children give equal time to all stimuli – touch, sound, vision, internal thoughts, and feelings. Their minds jump from one thing to the next. It is no wonder that these children are easily distracted, are unable to focus attention, are disorganized, are impulsive, and appear hyperactive. The inability to focus selective attention seems to be at the root of the problem.

Neurotransmitters

The attention center of the brain is turned off and on by chemicals. These chemicals are called neurotransmitters because they transmit information from one neuron to the next. Animal studies have suggested that injury to the attention center causes a decrease in neurotransmitters and is associated with ADD-like behavior in animals. Giving these research animals stimulant medication raises the level of neurotransmitters and allows the animals to function in a more normal way.

Neurotransmitters are formed from dietary proteins. Two common neurotransmitters found in the brain are norepinephrine and dopamine. They are catecholamines that are synthesized from the amino acid tyrosine. Medications that increase their availability to the central nervous system improve ADD symptoms in ADD children.

ADD children are felt to have a lack of neurotransmitters in their attention centers. Anything that affects the level of these chemicals could interfere with the attention center and thereby cause ADD-like symptoms. Diet and allergies can affect these chemicals in multiple ways and this might explain why a few ADD children are helped by changes in their diet. There are many other things that more directly affect the chemicals in the attention center.

Some Implications of These Findings

- Brainpower can be increased by providing a stimulating environment.
- The more mentally active a child is, the more connections he or she can make.
- Use it or lose it.
- Stay away from TV. Recent studies suggest that a child uses more energy reading a book than watching TV. If anything, TV teaches children to focus attention only when being entertained.

Insults to the Central Nervous System (CNS)

We are just now learning how complicated our brain and nervous systems are. As noted above, their function can be compromised by many factors. Insults to the nervous system can cause or aggravate ADD symptoms. It is important to study these insults because their study may lead to a better understanding of ADD problems and its biochemistry.

Diseases

Both acute and chronic diseases can affect our ability to concentrate. Encephalitis and spinal meningitis have been implicated as a possible cause of ADD in some children. These diseases are thought to cause damage to the brain, thereby causing the ADD symptoms. Any child with a chronic debilitating illness can develop ADD symptoms because of damage to the nervous system either directly from the disease or from our treatment of the disease.

Medical Treatment

Medical treatment of some illnesses can cause ADD problems. Recently studies on children who have had radiation treatment of the brain for leukemia have shown that these children may develop problems with learning and attention after radiation treatment.

Medications

Medications also have been shown to cause ADD-like behavior. Phenobarbital for seizures can cause irritableness and hyperactivity. Amminophyline, a common medication used in asthma, has been shown to cause inattention and hyperactivity in some children. Asthma medications that contain adrenalin-like compounds can cause hyperactivity. Steroids are another type of medication used in allergy conditions. These medications can cause irritability and inattention. Any medication has the potential of aggravating ADD symptoms.

Toxins

Exposure to certain chemicals has been shown to cause ADD symptoms. The most notable are lead, cocaine and alcohol. Lead exposure causes damage to the CNS and can cause problems with learning and attention. Recently research has shown that alcohol ingestion during pregnancy can cause damage to the baby. This is called Fetal Alcohol Syndrome (FAS) and is associated with certain physical findings along with ADD and learning problems.

Diet

In the Nineteen Seventies, a physician named Ben Feingold suggested that hyperactivity was caused by a reaction to what we eat. He proposed that artificial colorings, flavorings and naturally occurring chemicals called salicylates produce both learning disabilities and hyperactivity in most children who have ADD. Dr. Feingold's theory was very popular and he did much to promote it through the media. Many frustrated parents who had not been able to find other solutions for the problems of their children readily jumped on the bandwagon in the hope that this would be the answer.

In controlled studies where ADD children were put on the Feingold diet or a diet containing food additives, research showed only 5% of the children had sustained improvement on the Feingold diet as compared to the diet with food additives. It is interesting to note that 40% of the children seemed to improve initially on both the Feingold diet and the control diet (with food additives).

There are many reasons why the Feingold theory has remained popular in the United States even though research does not support its efficacy for most ADD children. The first is that it seems to help some children. As noted above, 40% of children appear to be helped when initiating the diet. The problem is that for many children this initial success is followed by a return of the ADD problems. Many continue the diet hoping that the benefits will return. In these children, the initial success was the result of a placebo effect rather than the actual diet.

Placebos are medications that have no active ingredients in them. They are used to determine if new medicines or treatments are effective. Patients are put on an active medicine to be evaluated or the placebo (inactive medicine). The patients are then tested to see if either the active or placebo helped the patient. Neither the patient nor the evaluator know which chemical the patient is using. Studies have shown that up to 40% of patients have an initial beneficial effect from the placebo. If the active medication does not help more than 40% of the patients it is considered not to be effective.

Research has shown that the mere suggestion that some intervention will help a problem can cause an apparent improvement in the problem. Many different interventions may produce short-term effects for different psychological, physical or behavioral disorders because the people employing them believe that they will help. The difficulty is that this improvement is not sustained and the old problems return. This short-lived effect is called the placebo effect. There is even evidence in some medical areas that the placebo effect may actually involve physical and chemical changes in the body. As noted above, the Feingold diet has not been shown to be effective for most ADD children.

Food Allergies

The second reason why Feingold associations may still proliferate is that there is a small percentage of children who may be diet sensitive. They may be allergic to the substances that Dr. Feingold identified or to other foods. Research on these types of allergies has suggested that they do not cause ADD but that they may aggravate the behavior. It is not unusual for parents to note that their child's behavior becomes much worse after the child has eaten a certain food. We also know that ADD children have more allergy symptoms (hay fever and asthma) than other children. This would suggest that the tendency towards allergies and ADD behaviors might be inherited and linked closely together in some individuals.

Sugar

Recent research on sugar has produced some rather interesting results, which make it important to keep in mind the distinction between hyperactivity and ADD. The research has suggested that the ingestion of large amounts of sugar or carbohydrates, unbalanced by any other types of food such as protein, will produce a reduction in hyperactivity and even lethargy, but it will also produce a decreased ability to concentrate. In a sense then, hyperactivity improves and ADD gets worse. It has been suggested that ADD children may crave sweets even more because they are unconsciously seeking something that might have a tranquilizing effect.

If sugar is not the cause of ADD and does not aggravate hyperactivity in most children, where did the idea come from that it does? One of the possible sources of this notion is that the situations in which children ingest a large amount of sugar are also situations that tend to be stimulating themselves. A birthday party or Halloween night may involve a good deal of excitement and social stimulation, which triggers the emotional over arousal and hyperactivity in the ADD child.

Implications

The ADD child is affected by his genetic constitution (nature) that causes a lack of neurotransmitters in the brain and this, in turn, is affected by his environment (nurture). When evaluating children for ADD problems, it is important to look at possible environmental insults to the brain that could be changed or removed (e.g., chronic medications). It is important to counsel families with ADD children to avoid lead exposures and for mothers to abstain from alcoholic beverages or illegal drugs during pregnancy. Science is just beginning to understand the relationship between ADD and the child's environment. In the future, we will be able to prevent some children from developing ADD symptoms by modifying their environment.

4

Prevention

Having ADD

- Does not mean that the child cannot learn
- Does not mean that the child cannot control behavior
- It's just more difficult
- It takes more time and effort to be successful
- Practice makes perfect – the ADD child needs to practice more than other children

Recently, more and more children are being diagnosed as having ADD. Is this because children are being misdiagnosed, or that kids who have previously been missed are being diagnosed, or that there is an increased incidence of ADD? Probably, all the above add to the increasing numbers of children being called ADD. Is there a way to prevent ADD problems from developing?

Prenatal Prevention

We know that there is an increased risk of developing ADD and learning disabilities when the fetus is exposed to certain environmental chemicals. We must let pregnant mothers know that they risk harming their future children by drinking alcohol, or using cocaine and other drugs during pregnancy. If we can insure good nutrition during pregnancy, there is less risk of prematurity. Premature infants are at risk for developing ADD and LD problems.

First Two Years

Many of the child's fundamental traits begin during the first two years of life. The parent can help prevent certain conditions that might lead to ADD symptoms by taking the child to routine health exams and providing some structure to the child's day.

Health exams are important for many reasons. Developmental delays in speech or motor skills can be spotted early and the child can be put in programs to improve these skills. Lead screening can be done to identify children with lead poisoning. Lead poisoning has been shown to cause ADD problems and learning problems. Immunizations can prevent some illnesses that could cause brain damage and ADD symptoms.

Parents can help prevent organizational problems from developing by providing structure for young children. Having a regular time for meals and bed are critical in helping the child learn a routine and have a concept of time. Children in very disorganized families appear to be very active and disorganized. Having a regular schedule and appropriate behavioral consequences helps the young child to become organized, attentive and less active.

Preschool

Attention

What did kids do before television? Many preschool children spend many hours a day in front of the TV. During this time the box is entertaining them. They are not exploring or interacting with others. The TV screen is constantly changing from one view to another. If anything, the TV teaches the child to be passively entertained by watching constantly changing visual images. During TV time the child is not learning about behavior nor about cause and effect. Is this why so many of today's children say they are bored? Are they bored or have they not learned to entertain themselves without TV?

It is interesting to note that in many Japanese day care settings children are taught to focus starting at age two. They sit in a group and are asked to focus on an object for increasing lengths of time. The children are rewarded by the teacher and by the other students when they can focus for certain lengths of time. The Japanese say they don't have children with ADD. Perhaps they are preventing some cases of ADD by teaching children to concentrate at a young age.

Organization

Everyone needs some sort of structure in life. ADD children do better with structure. If parents start helping the child to become organized at a young age, the ADD child will do better. This help can be given by developing routines for activities and setting specific times to do things. If a child plays with a game, the routine would be to pick up the game and put it away when done. It helps the ADD child if there is a routine time for meals and bedtime. Having routines to follow bring some structure to the ADD child's chaotic life.

Impulsive Behavior

Recent research suggests that children who are impulsive and cannot delay gratification have increased problems with life. ADD children by nature are impulsive. They act before they think and this gets them into all sorts of trouble socially and behaviorally. Parents need to actively work on teaching their ADD children to think before they act. This can be done by giving the child constant feedback. Praise is given for thinking and consequences are given for impulsive behavior. The key seems to be to work on this at an early age and devote a great deal of parental time to this activity. Again, ADD children can learn; it just takes time and effort on everyone's part.

School Age

Prepare for Learning

Set aside time for learning. Starting in infancy, read to the child every day. In kindergarten have a homework time (fifteen minutes where the child works on his letters or is read to). As the child approaches fourth grade, have a homework time that is always used. If the child has no homework from school, then he or she reads or keeps a journal. Since the child has to do some sort of work no matter what, there is an incentive to bring the schoolwork home.

Have chores for the child to do. Starting at four years of age the child should brush teeth, pick up toys and clothes, and learn to make the bed. Starting in kindergarten the child should help with tasks that benefit the entire family like setting the table or taking the garbage out. By doing these chores, the child is learning to become organized and responsible. As the child gets homework in school, it becomes just another chore to be done as part of life's routine.

Prevention of Writing Problems

Written language is the most difficult of all tasks that an individual has to learn. It requires more organization and attention to details than anything else we do. In writing a paragraph, the child must be able to form letters, spell, capitalize, punctuate, sequence, organize thoughts, structure sentences and the paragraph, etc. No wonder ADD children avoid writing like the plague.

Preventing writing problems revolves around the idea of having the child use oral abilities and the computer. Below are listed some ideas that will help with written work.

- Read daily with children. Discuss what happened in the chapters.
- Discuss current events with children by having them read the newspaper or watch the news on TV. Have them use paragraph format for their discussion. A topic sentence followed by several supporting facts and then a conclusion. The idea is to make this discussion fun for the child. The example that I use in the office: "I went to see Dr. Blair for school problems today. He is dumb and bald. He had a lot of dumb ideas to make me work harder. I never want to come back!" This helps expand children's knowledge base and helps them organize their thoughts.
- Have them write daily. Make it simple at first. Copy a couple of sentences. Have them dictate their thoughts to you and then they copy what you wrote down for them. Eventually, have them keep a journal of what happened during the day. Once a week look over the journal and correct spelling, grammar, and organization. This will help them develop report writing for school.
- If the school is not working on doing reports, have the child do reports at home by fourth grade. Reports should be done by first collecting information on note cards, making an outline of topics to be covered, doing a rough draft, and finally proofing the draft for spelling, grammar, etc.

- Teach the ADD child to type and use a computer for written work. Once the child learns to type at twenty words per minute, typing will be faster than writing by hand. The computer helps break the work down into segments without having to recopy the work ten times. See the chapter on dealing with schools for more ideas on use of computers.

Social Skills Training

Social skills are difficult for ADD children because they don't pay attention to the consequences of their behavior. ADD children don't notice other people's body language or facial expressions. Even if they do notice these nonverbal communications, they often don't process the information. This means these children do not modify their behavior in response to other people. Most people learn to respond to social cues by trial and error. Children with ADD must be taught social skills because they do not pay attention to the social cues of others.

It is important to work on social skills before age ten0 because children aren't as easy to train as they get close to the teenage years. The parent might attend parenting classes or social skill classes to get ideas on how to help an ADD child who is having problems with social skills. Again, a lot of time needs to be spent in this area by parents and school. Children need to be taught specific skills and then taught how to apply them to new and different situations.

Tutor

Every ADD child will need help at sometime because he or she wasn't tuned in for a particular subject at school. The tutor should work on the following:

- Work on organization
- Work on learning strategies – must relate to current schoolwork
- Work on coping strategies

Strengths – Don't Neglect

All children have strengths that can be developed. The ADD child doesn't often volunteer to work on skills. Once the ADD child figures out that working on skills requires sustained effort , such work will be avoided. Consequently, the parent has to push the child to work on areas that the child could be good in. Strengths need to be built so that the children can feel good about themselves and develop good self-esteem. When children feel good about themselves, they will have the energy to work on things that are difficult. If they have not developed a good self-esteem, they will not work on difficult things and they will either act out or drop out.

Involve ADD children in things that they like or are naturally good at. If they won't choose something to be involved in, give them a choice of three things to do. If they can't decide, you pick one and get them involved. They need to practice the activity on a daily basis. The younger the child starts to work on strengths or interests, the better he or she will become. It is usually much easier to motivate a younger child than an adolescent.

To do nothing—is never an option for the child!

Conclusion

There are many things that parents can do to help their ADD children become more successful. They need to find and build strengths in their children so that good self-esteem is developed. The parents should make the home a place where their children can learn about organization and structure. Lastly, ADD children need to practice things that will teach them to be attentive. Success leads to more success.

Hints:

- Teach children to focus on things.
- Look at a picture book with the child or work with the child to focus on an object like the Japanese do.
- After the child watches a TV program, discuss the program.
- Look for strengths to help build the child's self-esteem.
- Start working on behavior and social skills at a young age.

5

Recruiting the Team

African Proverb: It takes a village to raise a child.

Mrs. Smith had an ADD child named Jeff. When first seen, she was very depressed. She felt that she was a failure as a parent and as a mother. Jeff had been kicked out of nursery school and no baby-sitter would watch him. Mrs. Smith had tried everything in an attempt to control Jeff's impulsive and hyperactive behavior. Nothing had worked: not time-out, not scolding, not spanking. Jeff was at the emergency room several times a year and Mrs. Smith felt sure that she was going to be reported for child abuse. Mrs. Smith's family had told her she should be stricter and spend more time with Jeff.

ADD is a handicap that affects the child and family in many different ways. The child can have problems in school, at home and with peers. There is no one quick cure for the ADD child or family. It takes parental time and energy to help the ADD child reach his or her potential. The parents must recruit a team of professionals to help deal with the complicated and multifaceted problems that are created by the handicap.

The Captain Of The Team – Parent

The parents are the most important part of the team. They are the "captains of the ship" and must deal with "Jeff" on an everyday basis. They must find people to help "Jeff" succeed. They need to keep their "cool" even when stressed by the problems the ADD child has caused at home, at school, or in the community. They cannot afford to become depressed or lose control.

Grief

ADD is a handicapping condition that causes parents to grieve about the loss of the "ideal" child. Most parents go through the following stages of grieving at one time or another:

Denial

Parents with handicapped children initially deny that a problem exists. They feel that "Jeff will outgrow it" or that "It's just a stage he is going through." "How can this psychologist say I have an ADD child when he is perfect at home?" Usually after constant reminders from family, friends, and school, the parents begin to realize something is wrong.

Anger

Parents often become angry when confronted with a handicapping condition. They tend to take their anger out on other people. "Why should I have an ADD child? Why don't the drug abusing parents down the street have handicapped children instead of me?"

"I'm going to get that school. They don't know how to teach or handle children. It's their fault that Jeff is having problems in school." Actually, anger is healthy and can be helpful as a motivator towards action. Parents need to channel their actions so that they are beneficial to the child and not detrimental. Blaming teachers, schools, and others is not helpful in correcting the problem and is a waste of vital energy.

Guilt

All parents feel guilty when their children are not perfect. Certainly, ADD children are far from perfect and the parents often feel responsible for the child's problems. "If only I would have been firmer with him when he was two."

Unfortunately, there are no quick solutions to ADD problems. Most professionals feel that ADD is a biochemical problem rather than a parent-induced problem.

Depression

All parents of handicapped children become depressed at times. This is only natural. When parents have to deal with an overactive, inattentive child 24 hours a day, the job becomes overwhelming. Parents often exhaust all their resources in trying to help the child.

Acceptance

Acceptance is one of the last stages of grieving. It is a state where the parent realizes that the child has multiple problems. During this stage, the parents can channel their energies into constructive ways of helping the child and the family cope. Parents frequently bounce back and forth between acceptance and the other stages of grieving.

Hope

Throughout all of the stages of grieving the parents hope that the child will recover from or overcome the handicap. This is the force that keeps parents trying to help the ADD child even when things seem bleak. "Without hope, we are lost."

Parents cannot handle the multitude of problems by themselves. They need help in dealing with the handicap and the grieving process as outlined above. How do you find someone to help?

Marital Stress – Fathers

Fathers deserve special attention. It has been the custom in the United States for mothers to bear the responsibility for managing the handicapped child. Fathers tend to drop out of the management because they don't know what is going on. Frequently, mothers become angry because of the frustrations of trying to handle a multitude of duties (work, household chores, and the ADD child) by themselves. The fathers may feel that the mothers are ineffective as parents because the ADD child usually responds better to men.

Studies have shown this response is more related to the physical size and deeper voice of the male.

Suggestion for mothers: All mothers should feign illness for one week and delegate all maternal duties to the father. The mother must resist all temptations to help Dad or the children. This will help the father to understand the mother's problems and will lead to an appreciation of Mom!!

There is nothing worse for either parent than to come home to a chaotic household with the children completely out of control. The parent who has worked all day then has to try to calm the family down. As a consequence, many parents find their work more rewarding than their home, so they start working longer hours rather than dealing with solutions for the home problems. This is unfair to the other parent who is left with all the responsibilities. It's no wonder that many marriages fall apart with the added stress of an ADD child.

Prevention of Marital Stress

- Both mother and father should have at least one half day off a week while the other parent manages the household.
- The parents should spend several hours together without the kids doing something they both enjoy doing.
- Dad should be kept involved in the treatment program for the child (e.g. school conferences).
- Both parents should recognize each other's strengths and give "strokes" for jobs well done.
- Single parents need to follow the above rules and find support people to help them manage the family.

Other Members of the Team

Which professional to see? It would be wonderful if one professional was an expert in the educational, behavioral, social and medical problems of the ADD child. In reality, that person doesn't exist. One person wouldn't have the necessary time or energy to deal with all the problems. Therefore, the parent is going to need to see several professionals.

Psychologists

Many parents need professional help to deal with grief. Usually a psychologist or counselor can be of help. These professionals should be family oriented. ADD is a family problem and the professional should be able to help the parents with their grieving reactions. They should give the family concrete suggestions on dealing with behavioral problems.

They should also help the ADD child develop better self-esteem and help siblings cope with the ADD child's intrusive behavior.

Psychologists can make the diagnosis of ADD. They can help counsel the family and child on the problems associated with ADD. During times of stress and crises, psychologists can be invaluable in helping to find solutions for problems.

They cannot prescribe medication for ADD problems.

Physicians

Family physicians, pediatricians, behavioral pediatricians, pediatric neurologists, and psychiatrists can diagnose and prescribe medication for ADD children. Asking the physician the questions outlined at the end of this chapter will increase the chances of finding the best physician to help the ADD child.

School Personnel

ADD children spend a majority of their day in school. The parent must find someone to be the child's advocate at the school. This could be a teacher, a social worker, a school psychologist, or a principal. It would be helpful if that person was knowledgeable about ADD, but the most important attribute is a caring attitude for the child. ADD children often need extra help in the school situation. Having an advocate for your child within the system makes dealing with the school much easier. When you find that special advocate, be sure to reward him or her with praise and thanks. Remember that these special people get no monetary remuneration for extra effort. Their best reward is seeing the child succeed.

Tutors

Forty percent of ADD children have associated learning disabilities. These children require more help than the school can provide. They can benefit from individualized tutoring and often learn more in one hour of one-on-one than they do in a week of regular classes at school. Even ADD children without specific learning disabilities will often need tutoring in subjects that do not interest them.

Support Groups

Support groups can be very beneficial for ADD parents. They can serve as a resource for information and provide emotional support. Knowing that you are not the only one facing a difficult problem can help. These groups can serve as a source of hope that there are answers to the ADD problem. As noted above, they can give information to parents about knowledgeable psychologists, physicians, and teachers.

The Family

Many times ADD children become the focus of the family. They certainly require more time than the other children. Parents can easily neglect the other less demanding children. Over time, this neglect can lead to jealousy and resentment in the other children.

It is very important to explain this handicap to the other children and make them part of the team. Enlist their help. Older sibs can read to or with the ADD child. The sibling can then share in the ADD child's success in reading. Try to use consistent behavioral management with all the children. Take time to praise the other children for helping the ADD child overcome problems. See the chapters on behavioral management.

A Mentor

Try to find an adult who can become a mentor for the child. Having an adult to talk to who is not a part of the immediate family can be of great help to the ADD child. This adult can give advice and praise for success that is not compromised by being the child's parent.

The ADD Child

Parents often forget about making the ADD child part of the team. This can be accomplished by explaining ADD in simple terms to the child, allowing the child to have some input into decisions and giving the child choices whenever possible. Preparing the child to attend school conferences and participate in decisions gives the child some control and power over his or her life. Children who have been prepared in this way usually have a much easier time during adolescence.

Conclusion

ADD children require more parental energy than do other members of the family. The parents only have a limited amount of time and energy to expend on the ADD child, so it is important for them to find good outside resources to help. They must learn to utilize these resources in an effective way. If the parents can manage this difficult task, all the members of the family can benefit and learn to be successful in the face of adversity.

How to Find the Right Professional?

Ask friends, colleagues, teachers and support groups for references. The following is a list of questions that might help determine how knowledgeable a professional is in the field of ADD treatment.

- Have you treated many ADD children?
- Do you have handouts for parents on ADD and associated problems?
- Do you use checklists for home and school to monitor problems?
- Do you call teachers and physicians when there are problems?
- What are your charges?
- How often do you want to see the child?
- Do you give written reports of your findings and therapy?
- Do you believe medication can be helpful in the treatment of ADD?
- How available are you in case of crises?

Questions to ask yourself after talking with the professional:

- Did you feel comfortable with the professional?
- Did he or she seem knowledgeable about ADD issues?
- Was the professional sympathetic and empathetic?

6
"TEACH" and the Win-Win Approach

Teaching Behavior to Children

This chapter is not meant to be a comprehensive guide to behavioral management but it is intended to give general guidelines to parents on managing behavior in ADD children. ADD children challenge even the most patient of parents. This is because they are impulsive and don't pay attention to the consequences of their behavior. All behavioral strategies are based on the need for the child to think before acting; therefore, it takes more effort and practice for the ADD child to become successful behaviorally. The steps that are needed can be expressed in the acronym TEACH. There are innumerable books written on behavioral management in children. The reader is referred to the bibliography at the end of this book for more comprehensive resources on behavioral management.

The Basics

There are four concepts that are important to understand when discussing behavior and ADD children.

First, children are not born with a sense of right and wrong but learn from their parents what is acceptable. Children soon learn it is not a good idea to touch a hot stove because this is a painful experience.

Second, children generally want to please their parents but will settle for negative attention if they find that is the only type of attention they are capable of earning.

Third, ADD children are slow at learning good behavior because they don't pay attention to cause and effect; they are impulsive and they find it easier to get negative parental attention than to get positive parental attention.

Fourth, a positive environment will help the child do better behaviorally.

These four concepts mandate that parents be patient and wise teachers if they want their ADD children to become successful behaviorally.

TEACH

T - Time

There are two concepts involving time and behavior. The first concept is that it takes time to change behavior. The second concept is that many behaviors reoccur at predictable times.

The number one reason most parents have difficulty correcting problem behavior is that they don't set aside enough time. They try to correct Jeff's behavior at the grocery store when they are in a rush. Jeff knows this and usually gets away with the behavior because the parent doesn't have time to deal with it.

Most parents want to be able to tell children what they should do and expect them to do it; however, this is not reasonable. If an adult was learning to bowl for the first time, the teacher would expect him or her to throw many gutter balls before throwing strikes. The teacher realizes the bowler knows what to do but getting ones body to do it requires a lot of time and practice. Learning new behavior also requires time and practice.

The parents should observe if there are specific times when the child is having behavior problems. Changing the circumstance at these times can often change the behavior. If the child's behavior deteriorates when tired, the solution is for the child to get more rest. If the child only misbehaves when around a certain hyperactive child, avoid that child. If he or she always causes problems when parents are getting dinner ready, try to find something fun for the child to do at that time.

Hints:

- Don't work on behavior when you have other commitments that need to be done now.

- Work on one behavior at a time or you will become overwhelmed and defeated.

- By noting the time when the child is misbehaving we often can figure out a way to prevent recurrences of the behavior.

E - Expectations

It is important to set clear behavioral expectations for ADD children. The parent must be as consistent as possible because of the child's inattention and impulsivity. Otherwise, the child will not learn what is expected. Make instructions simple and don't expect too much. Remember it takes time and energy to change behavior. Look for improvements and praise the child for them.

Try not to remind the child repeatedly not to do something. Behavioral research has shown that reminding someone not to do something is more likely to make the behavior worse than to improve it. Think what you would do if you were asked not to look for red cars when driving. None of us like to be told not to do something and our first reaction is to not follow the direction. Our mind has only one picture in it and that is of a red car so that it is very difficult to avoid noticing red cars. This is exactly what happens when Jeff is told not to touch the birthday cake. The child becomes focused on the cake and can't keep from touching it because of impulsiveness. Paint the picture you want to see and avoid the "don't" word. In the birthday cake episode, the parent could ask the child to help set the table rather than bringing the cake to the child's attention.

Parents often expect that their children will misbehave in certain situations. Expectations often become reality. This is because parents treat children differently if they expect bad behavior rather than good behavior. If parents are expecting good behavior, they often will ignore inappropriate behavior and notice the positive behaviors in the child. Giving attention to any type of behavior is a great reinforcer of that behavior be it good or bad. Parents need to change their expectation to, "My child will learn to behave!"

Hints:

- Expect the child to be good.
- Don't remind.

A - Attitude

Parents need to have a positive, can do attitude when dealing with ADD children. This is easier said than done when the parent has had a bad day at work and comes home to the chaos that an ADD child can create. The parent needs to have the positive attitude of a good coach. The coach knows that the kids will make mistakes but encourages them to keep trying and improving. This is a much better attitude than the negative coach who is always angry and demeaning.

The child is in control when parents become angry. If the child says, "I'm sorry." our anger subsides but if the child says, "You can't make me do it!" our anger increases. Many kids are power-mongers and take delight in making their parents go stark raving mad even though they risk getting disciplined. It's fun to drive someone over the edge. Don't deal with bad behavior when you are angry. Send them to their rooms until you get control.

One way of helping yourself develop a positive attitude is to use visual imagery. Coaches have for years taught athletes to visualize themselves hitting or catching the ball. To the mind, visualizing something happening is almost as good as doing the real thing. Practice makes perfect and visualizing is a type of practice that will help the parent perform with a positive attitude.

The steps of developing a positive coaching attitude by using visual imagery:

- Picture the child behaving poorly in a typical situation.
- Picture yourself being calm and using a consequence for the behavior.
- Imagine the child accepting the consequence without too much fuss.
- Picture yourself giving positive encouragement - not a lecture. "I know you will do better next time," rather than, "I told you you would be grounded for a year if you did it again."

- Picture the child being in a similar situation and behaving appropriately the next time.
- Praise the child for the good behavior.
- Picture the smile on the child's face and your own.

Parents need to look at their own attitude towards the child. If the parent doesn't like the child or quickly becomes angry with the child's behavior, that parent will not be effective. If the parent cannot overcome these feelings towards the child with imagery and by focusing on the child's positives, then professional help is needed to look at the causes of the feelings. See the chapter on Recruiting the Team.

Many parents feel guilty about having a child who has problems. They feel that they have caused the problems or they are burned out from dealing with all the problems of having an ADD child. They consequently let the child get by without setting consistent behavior guidelines. Some parents are handicapped because of their own upbringing and find it difficult to use time-out or other consequences because of a fear that the child won't love them. Other parents who were brought up in homes where the parents were either physically or emotionally abusive find it hard to use positive behavioral techniques. These parents, when stressed, tend to revert to the abusive techniques that were used by their own parents. Remember children feel more comfortable if they know that they are loved and know what the limits and expectations are.

Hints:

- Don't discipline when angry – it doesn't work.
- Use visual imagery to develop more effective discipline.
- If you find it hard to develop a positive attitude toward your child, get help.

C - Consequence

Children will behave if it is worthwhile for them to behave. The trick is to find strategies that make it worthwhile for them to control their own behavior. In simple terms, there are only two methods of changing behavior. Children can be rewarded for appropriate behaviors (bribing), or they can suffer consequences for inappropriate behavior (loss of privileges).

The most effective reward is positive parental attention and praise. As discussed above children crave positive adult attention. So be sure to catch the child doing something right and praise him or her for the good behavior. This is very hard to do when the child has had a bad day, but search for something positive, no matter how small. Positive attention is effective in helping improve behavior.

There are many other rewards that can be used to motivate a child to work on improving behavior. See the list in the chapter on Behavioral and Educational Strategies – School.

When parents set up consequences for behavior they must strive to be consistent. There is nothing more anxiety provoking for the child than having a parent be lenient sometimes and harsh at other times. The child doesn't know what to expect and becomes confused and anxious. When a child has a handicap like ADD, it is hard for the parent to be consistent and take action every time something goes wrong; therefore, it is important to pick the most important behaviors to work on. A consistent behavior program can then be set up for those few behaviors that are key to making family life happy.

Keeping Score – Contracts and Charts

Many children like the idea of contracts because it makes things official. No one can argue about what was agreed on if there is a contract that is signed by both parties. Children often feel that parents only remember the negative consequences for behavior and forget the reward aspects. Keeping a chart of how things are going in plain view for all to behold also helps the child because it serves as a visual cue. See chapter seven on Behavior Problems for an example of charting.

Consequences

The easiest of consequence to use is time-out: The child is told to stop or he or she will have to sit on a chair or go to the bedroom. This removes the child from the situation and allows everyone to calm down. If the bedroom is used, it puts the child in an area where there is less likelihood of getting into trouble. When calm, the child is allowed to come out. Attention is then given for being in control rather than negative attention being given for out of control behavior.

Spanking is not very effective in teaching children appropriate behavior. If parents spank when they are angry, it teaches the children to hit when angry. Some authorities believe it is okay to spank children occasionally; however, if a child needs to be spanked over and over again for the same behavior, then spanking is not working and some other means of discipline should be used. If the ADD child is aggressive, spanking should not be used because it makes the child more aggressive.

In general, removing privileges is much more effective in teaching behavior than spanking. Telling children they may not watch TV, go outside, talk on the phone, play the computer, or eat until the chores are done can be very effective in getting their cooperation. The trick is to make it worthwhile for children to control behavior. If the children learn that privileges and parental attention are given for controlling behavior, they will quickly learn control.

Parents should try to make consequences a win-win situation. For sibling fighting, the children are told if they fight they will get to do chores together. This way the parent will either have the cleanest house in town or the kids will learn to negotiate arguments.

Too often we make all-or-none behavioral demands on children. We don't notice the child has improved a little. If a child's behavior is improving slowly towards the goal of good behavior, we should recognize the incremental improvement. "You are doing a lot better today." Remember, reminding someone of his or her behavior actually reinforces the behavior. Reminding a child about improvement in behavior reinforces the concept of improvement.

Hints:

- Positive parental attention is the most effective behavioral motivator that there is.
- Work on only a few behaviors at a time.
- Be consistent – it's easier said than done.
- Look for improvement not perfection.
- Remind the child of improvements not of mistakes.

H - Help

Even the best of parents needs help in dealing with the ADD child. The ADD child requires four to five times the energy of an average child. The parent has to keep a couple of steps ahead of the child or the child will never make progress in the right direction. The parent needs to recruit a team to help with behavior and other problems that the ADD child has. No one person can have all the answers. See the chapter on Recruiting the Team.

Help the child by controlling the child's environment. Make sure the child is getting enough rest. Tired children tend to be cranky children. If a child has trouble in unsupervised time, try to provide some supervision. Set up situations where you have the time and energy to work on behavior. Help the child become successful by finding areas that the child likes and can succeed in. Success builds self-esteem and good self-esteem usually means better behavior.

Hints:

- Recruit a team to help the child succeed.
- Make the child's environment conducive to success.

Conclusion

Children are not born with a sense of what is right and wrong. They learn over time what is acceptable behavior. ADD children, because of their problems with attention and impulsivity, don't learn as quickly as other children. It is actually easier for them to learn how to get negative attention for bad behavior than to learn how to get positive attention for appropriate behavior. It takes a maximum effort on the part of parents to TEACH their ADD children good behavior. It is worth the struggle!

The Win-Win Approach

I guess I am an eternal optimist. In dealing with children over the years, I am always impressed with how children respond to positive strokes. They crave this type of attention. However, if they don't get positive attention they will settle for negative attention. Any type of attention is better than no attention at all!

The Behavior Game

Behavior is a contest between the child's tendencies to want to be independent and recognized (good or bad recognition) and the parents' desire to have the child learn society's rules and behave appropriately. Needless to say, children with ADD find it easier to get the negative recognition. After awhile this negative recognition leads to negative behaviors – acting out or dropping out.

Change is Difficult and Requires a Lot of Energy

Everyone becomes comfortable with the status quo. We know what to expect and how to react. We are creatures of habit. Adults find it very difficult to change their golf swing or to learn a new way of doing a task. To help a child change requires an enormous amount of effort and patience on the part of the adult. The adult must learn to change the way he or she responds to a child's inappropriate behavior or the child will continue the same old behavior. The child will try to throw roadblocks at the parent – to get back to the old game that is more comfortable even though it is painful.

The Individual Must be Motivated to Change

The key to successfully changing a child's behavior is to motivate the child to try a change. The parent or teacher can't make the child change his or her behavior. However, the parent can make it worthwhile for the child to attempt to change. There are only two ways to motivate a child:

- The first is to reward the behavior that we want to see happen. This is a perfectly acceptable method of changing behavior. Businesses use this technique all the time to reward outstanding performance. However, they only reward *improved* performance not the status quo. Rewards are very helpful in motivating a child to change behavior. They are not as helpful in sustaining appropriate behavior.
- The second method for motivating a child to change a behavior is to use consequences. Consequences can be either the removal of privileges (can't go outside, watch TV, use the phone, use the computer or eat until the job is done) or the assigning of an extra task (chore). The key is that it costs the child more to do things the wrong way than to do them the right way.

Traps

Children tend to fulfill their parents' expectation. What kind of picture are we painting? Parents need to be very careful about what messages they are sending to their children.

- **Power Game: "I'll make him do it!"** In a game of power the child has nothing to lose while the adult has dignity at stake. The child finds it fun to have the power to drive a parent over the edge. The parent, therefore, needs to avoid the power game and concentrate on a game that the adult can win.
- **Reminders:** In behavioral terms, reminding someone **not** to do something reinforces the behavior that is not wanted.
  - **Pictures:** The brain tends to use images. If an adult is told **not** to look for red cars on the drive home, his or her mind becomes focused on red cars and it becomes impossible not to notice red cars. When a child is reminded **not** to do something, the child's brain tends to ignore the "not" and paints a picture of the child doing the forbidden thing.

    We have learned from sports psychology that picturing yourself hitting the ball is almost as good as taking batting practice. Practice makes perfect whether it is mental practice or physical practice. Often when a child is reminded **not** to do something, the reminder paints a mental image of the child doing this thing. The image becomes a mental practice and makes it more likely that the child will do the wrong thing.
  - **Pushing:** If pushed to do something, a child either resists or pushes back. Reminders are a type of pushing. When you push a child to get going in the morning for school, he or she often moves slower with each reminder.
  - **Whose Brain?** We have talked about the importance of using it or losing it. When a child is reminded to do something, the parent is doing the thinking and the child is not having to use his or her brain. Try giving the child a hint, "Did you forget something?" or "Check your list." instead of spoon-feeding by saying, "Pick up your toys."
  - **Self-Esteem:** When you remind your child to do something, you are really saying that you don't think the child is capable

of remembering what to do. Over time this has a tendency to lower self-esteem.

Strategies

- **Paint the Right Picture:** Parents need to paint the picture that they want the child to see, not the one they want to change (as in the red car example). "Look at all the orange cars." Then the child doesn't notice the red cars. Red car: "Don't hit your sister." Orange car: "Help your sister with her coat."
- **Partial Reminders:** Parents should try to give their child hints rather than total reminders. Ask questions like, "Have you forgotten something?" or "Did you check your list?" These types of questions make the child think and, if he or she remembers, allows the parents to praise the child for remembering.

Concepts

- **Find the Positive:** There is usually something positive in any behavior. The parent has to be creative in finding that positive. If the child doesn't bring homework home, that means there will be plenty of time to work on other educationally related topics. If fights with siblings occur all the time, that means the child has lots of energy that can be spent on cleaning. If the child is impulsive and can't wait, it means he or she has lots of energy and can work on chores or some other activity.
- **Build Self-Esteem:** Children with ADD usually develop poor self-esteem because someone is always criticizing their schoolwork or their behavior. They get few positive strokes and often feel like they are a failure in the game of life. Reminders and corrections lower self-esteem. The child feels stupid because someone else has to tell him or her what to do. The trick in motivating a child is to set up situations in which the child gets positive strokes no matter what. This helps raise self-esteem and makes the child want to try harder.
- **Make Sure the Parent Wins:** Children won't play games in which they lose all the time and in which they have to do something that is not fun, especially if the opponent (the parent) is having a wonderful time.

Behavioral Game Plan

- Rules should be structured so that the parent wins no matter what the child does behaviorally.
- The child has a choice: Do what is appropriate or volunteer for slave labor.
- The parent doesn't care which one the child chooses to do. This removes any power that the child has to upset the parent. (The child will learn appropriate behavior or the parent will get the house cleaned.)
- The parent praises the child for doing either task – a positive picture. This helps build the child's self-esteem. When confronted with a losing situation people choose the least painful alternative. If the child chooses slave labor, he or she might be motivated at some time to try appropriate behavior to see if it is less painful.

Poop Scooper

Behavioral training is a dirty job but someone has to do it. This is a method of using some of the concepts discussed above to help parents deal with behavioral problems. This technique has proven helpful in dealing with some difficult behavior. Each letter in the name represents a step to be taken.

- **Positive:** Make a **p**ositive out of a negative. "It's great that you don't have any homework because I have something better for you to do, now that you have spare time."
- **Obligation:** As a parent you feel **o**bligated to provide the child with an opportunity to be successful. Therefore, the child gets to copy two pages out of the encyclopedia on any topic he or she likes. What a neat opportunity for the child to learn probably better than anything the school can come up with. The child gets to choose the topic. If homework is never brought home, the child will have read and copied the whole encyclopedia by the time he or she finishes high school!
- **Opportunity:** The parent acts enthusiastically about this new **o**pportunity and hopes that the child will choose the encyclopedia over doing homework. This change in parental behavior removes the child's ability to drive the parent over the edge. (When I ask kids if they have ever **not** turned in homework that their parents

have pushed them to do, the answer is almost universally yes. When I ask them what effect this has on their parents, the answer is that it drives their parents crazy. When I ask the children if it's fun to drive their parents crazy, they don't answer but just smile! The parents begin to realize that their attempts to push the child have led to the child pushing back – and to the child winning the pushing game because he or she has nothing to lose and the parents have their self-esteem and dignity at stake.)

- Praise the child for accomplishing the task (copying from the encyclopedia). Positive attention for doing something positive builds self-esteem. Probably the child will want to change this painful picture to one that doesn't require that obnoxious task to be completed. (The least painful alternative is to get organized and get the homework done and turned in.) If homework is done, the parent praises the child for accomplishing this difficult task.
- Smile, you are winning the game.
- Consequences will be needed, as the child will try to change the game back to the old way of doing things. If the child refuses to do either task (the assigned homework or copying pages from the encyclopedia), you don't care, but the child can't possibly go outside, watch TV, talk on the phone, or eat until one of the things is done.
- You still feel Obligated to provide the child with this wonderful Opportunity.
- Praise the child for accomplishing the task.
- Expect that the child will cooperate because there is no other choice.
- Relax – both you and the child have succeeded.

Examples of WIN-WIN

Sibling Fighting

Sibling fighting is a common occurrence in all families. Most of the time we have no idea who started the fight. Often the child we have labeled as the problem child will start the fight. However, just as often the good child will needle the problem child just enough to get a fight going.

When does the fighting occur? Usually, it is when the adult is trying to get something done, such as talk on the phone or to a neighbor. Fighting also occurs when the children are bored or have nothing to do.

Many times our attempts to stop the fighting make it worse. When we scold one of the children for fighting, that child feels like a loser and the other child feels like a winner. Unfortunately, both children will want to play the game again to see who will win the next time. Separating the children does not teach them to get along any better.

There is an old saying that, "Pressure from without brings unity from within." If adults are having minor problems with neighbors, these problems are soon forgotten if the city says that they are going to build a garbage dump across the street. The adults will band together to fight off the city and the minor problems will soon be forgotten.

The same concept can be used to stop sibling fighting. Try the Poop Scooper Technique.

- Make a **positive** out of a negative. "You guys sure have a lot of energy, but fighting isn't the most productive use of that energy."
- "I feel **obligated** to give you a better **opportunity**." Tell the children that you want them to fight! (This will throw them off guard – it's not what parents are supposed to say.) When children fight they are obviously bored and need something better to do with their time.
    - Since they are bored, you have multiple chores for them to do whenever they fight. They are to do these chores together

(teaches cooperation). If they continue to fight, so much the better because you have more chores that need to be done. Find chores that have a door between you and the children so you cannot see them (e.g., clean the bathroom or garage).
- Neither child can do anything until the chore is done and inspected by you.
- **Praise** the kids for accomplishing the task or stopping fighting.
- No matter what happens, keep **smiling**! You can't lose. You will have either the cleanest house on the block or the kids will learn to resolve their differences.
- **Consequences**: The children will try to manipulate you by saying that the other sib isn't helping. You say, "I don't care."
  - You don't care whether one child does all the work or they cooperate. If one child gets stuck with doing all the work, he or she will find a way to avoid a fight in the future.
  - Neither child can do anything until the job is done and inspected (can't go outside, watch TV, play the computer, eat, etc.).
- If they keep fighting, you are **obligated** to give them more cleaning **opportunities**.
- **Praise** the children for cooperating and for volunteering to clean. They are getting positive attention for either cooperating or for cleaning. They can't lose and neither can you.
- **Expect** that the children will learn the lesson quickly.
- **Relax** – the children are learning and both you and the children are winning.

The Concept of Over Correction

ADD children often display annoying habits like clearing their throat or making other noises by humming or tapping things. They are often unaware that their behavior is upsetting other people. As mentioned above, reminding children not to do something only reinforces the behavior. Over correction can help them stop the behavior.

Psychologist have used over correction for years to try and change undesirable behaviors. It is especially good for annoying habits. Over correction is an attempt to create self-awareness of the habit and to motivate the child to control it. Each time the ADD child does the behavior; he or she is asked to repeat the habit ten times. After a while the child becomes tired of having to repeat the habit over and over again and tries to suppress the urge to repeat the habit. This also can work for mild tics.

This technique can also be used when children forget to do a task. The child is told that practice makes perfect. Since he or she couldn't remember to put the dishes away, you feel obligated to provide a practice opportunity. All dishes are taken out of cupboard and replaced three times. As noted under the Poop Scooper technique, the child is not likely to opt for this opportunity again. Remember to keep a smile on your face!

7
Behavioral Problems

This chapter is intended to give parents specific ideas on how to handle problems at home. The child spends more hours at home than anywhere else. The first part of this chapter will look at the components of ADD that affect the child in the home. The last part of the chapter will deal with common behavioral problems.

Components of ADD

Attention

Difficulty paying attention is one of the core problems of ADD children. The attention center in these children is not turned on as well as it should be. They have problems with focusing attention and with being distracted. The trick is to try and get the ADD child to use the attention center. This not an easy task because most people avoid things that are difficult for them. As with any problem area, practice makes perfect. The question is how to motivate the ADD child to practice using attention.

Making things fun is one way to get children to practice. In younger children playing games like memory or Simon says requires them to pay attention. In older children, instruction in martial arts can be of benefit. With martial arts training, it is important to have an instructor who emphasizes self-control and discipline so that the child does not use new skills on other children.

The Japanese has used teaching focusing skills by meditating for centuries. They claim that they don't have ADD in their population.

Perhaps their early emphasis on learning to focus one's attention remediates an attention problem before it is noticed or classified as ADD. Some recent studies have suggested that learning to meditate can help ADD children to be more focused in the classroom. While this research is preliminary, it would confirm the Japanese experience. We can teach children to focus on objects or pictures by rewarding them for staying tuned into the object for increasingly longer periods of time. For example, several prizes could be purchased and when the child can sit still and focus on an object for thirty seconds he or she will receive a reward. The child will need to be able to focus for sixty seconds for the next prize. The world of the ADD child is full of "boring things" that have to be focused on and practice will help the child deal with this need.

Hyperactivity

The best strategy for dealing with hyperactivity at home is to provide the child outlets for energy. After school allow the child to go out and play. Swimming, soccer and other sports are good ways to burn up excessive energy. Give the child tasks that require movement rather than sitting. If the child has chores, pick chores that require movement like emptying the wastepaper baskets or picking up things in the yard. A home exercise program for the child and adult is beneficial for both. The child burns up energy and becomes physically healthier and the parent loses extra pounds. When choosing activities, make sure that the child can have fun and be successful in them.

Organization

Many ADD children have significant problems with organizing anything. The parent needs to help the child find strategies for dealing with this problem. The basic problem is that ADD children don't think organization is a priority. They would much rather go with the flow and experience things as they happen. They also would rather do only those things that are fun and easy. Parents must make organization a priority for them. Initially, a parent will need to organize the ADD child and then gradually back out and let the child sink or swim.

The sooner the child starts learning about organization the better off he or she will be. Children can be taught to pick up and put things in their proper place starting at eighteen months of age. As children approach four years of age they should be given chores to do. At this age, the self-help chores of picking up toys and clothes, getting dressed, brushing teeth, and making the bed should be emphasized. At ages five or six the child can start doing chores that help the whole family like setting the table or emptying the wastepaper baskets. To accomplish the chores the child will have to become organized.

The "list" is the most common organizer. For preschool children, a picture list can be made of the chores. For older children a written list can be used. Many children with ADD don't pay attention to time concepts and marking a calendar with chores can help them focus on the chores and the days of the week when things need to be done.

How do you get ADD children to make organization a priority? The answer is to make it worthwhile for them to become organized. The most effective method is to use consequences. They can't go outside, watch TV, play with the computer, talk on the phone or eat until their chores are done!

Hints:

- Don't remind children to do something over and over again.
- If they don't remember what they were supposed to do, have them check their list.
- Then praise them for finding the right task to complete rather than criticizing them for forgetting.
- See the Chapter on "Teach" for a discussion of the problems with reminding children to do something.

Impulsive Behavior

Impulsive behavior is very difficult to deal with because the child doesn't think before acting. This can cause all sorts of problems. The most serious problem is that the child will get hurt when running out into the street or some other impulsive action. Many children have social problems because they say aloud what they think rather than just thinking it. The parent must set up teaching situations and then be consistent with praise and consequences. For example, the child can be taught not to run into the street by stating that if the child crosses the sidewalk he or she will have to come inside for an hour. The parent then pretends not to be watching and takes the child inside if the sidewalk is crossed.

Teaching the child self-talk can help the child be less impulsive. Initially, the parent has the child tell orally how a specific problem should be handled. Once the child good at doing this, the parent asks the child to do it on all problems that are encountered. The parent rewards the child with praise for doing this and holds up a hand to stop the child if he or she starts to do something without first verbalizing how it should be done. The parent also notices improvement and encourages the child to keep trying. When the child has been successful over a period of time, the parent asks the child to think about what to do before acting rather than discussing it with the parent. If the child appears to think before acting, the child is rewarded.

We have found the win-win approach to be helpful with impulsive behavior at home and in school. If a child constantly interrupts an adult, this means he or she has lots of energy that is being used inappropriately. Therefore, the child needs to do something with the excess energy. The parent is obligated to give the child an opportunity to use that energy in a more positive way. Copying a paragraph or doing a chore for each interruption soon teaches the child to control his or her impulses. The child gets positive recognition for doing the paragraph, chore or for controlling the impulses.

Strategies

Charting

Charting behavior can help ADD children monitor their behavior. Many times ADD children are oblivious to the consequences of their actions. Having ADD children chart their behavior gives them visual feedback about how they are progressing. They can see improvement and are required to notice what their behavior has been.

Charts can be simple or complex. Simple charts look at one particular behavior and a star is given for appropriate behavior. More complex charts can record multiple behaviors and include both good behavior and inappropriate behavior. Most charts are tied to a reward system where the child earns stars for appropriate behavior and loses stars for the bad behavior. After a period of time, stars can be redeemed for a reward of some kind.

One concept that we have found to be very useful is to tie appropriate behavior to earning time doing a favorite activity. This can be very helpful in getting children to do chores. The child gets a check for each chore done in the morning. Each check is worth fifteen minutes of time doing an activity like playing the computer, watching TV, or playing outside.

Once the child is being successful, the charting is gradually removed. If the child reverts back to not doing the chores, the charting can be reinstituted or another strategy can be tried.

An example of a simple chart: Each time the child does something wrong (e.g., hits a sibling or blurts out something), he or she is asked to go put a checkmark on a piece of paper on the refrigerator. When the child gets three checks, he or she gets a ten minute time-out. The child soon gets tired of having to get up and mark the paper and this is especially helpful for impulsive behavior.

See an example of a more complex chart for chores on the next page:

Chart for Earning TV Time

Child's Name: _____

Place a check mark by each accomplished task

After school add up the number of checks

Each check is worth fifteen minutes of time watching TV

	Mon	Tues	Wed	Thur	Fri	Sat	Sun
Get Up After First Call							
Make Bed							
Brush Teeth							
Comb Hair							
Total Check Marks							

Self-Esteem

One of the most important things to protect is a child's self-esteem. A child who has a positive self-esteem can overcome immeasurable obstacles and become successful in the game called life. A child who feels good about himself or herself will have the energy to learn and try again. This child will develop positive self-talk and will feel that trying hard can bring success. The child can accept mistakes and will try again. He or she feels in control of the environment.

Those children who have low self-esteem tend to feel that they have no control over what is happening to them. They feel impotent. They deal with their difficulties by avoiding their problems. This leads to maladaptive strategies that are an attempt to protect themselves from being hurt. The two most often used strategies are dropping out or acting out. All children want to be recognized for something. Children who act out and get into trouble gain recognition for being troublemakers. They feel that this is an easier way to be recognized than trying to deal with rules at home and school.

It is easy to see how children with ADD can develop poor self-esteem. The child's core problems of inattention, hyperactivity, impulsive behavior and poor social skills lead to difficulties at home, in school and with peers. About one third of ADD children have coordination problems and another third have learning disabilities. It is easy for them to become the focus of negative attention from peers and adults because of their behavior. Special effort is needed to help the ADD child develop positive self-esteem.

Building Self-Esteem

The parent of the ADD child needs to understand several basic concepts about human nature that affect self-esteem.

All children need to feel needed and that they are important to family, friends and school. ADD children have problems with self-esteem because they are often criticized for behavior and grades. They often feel that their family would be better off without them. The trick is for the parent and the school to make the child feel needed. All children, no matter how bad they are, have some redeeming characteristics. The parent and school must find those characteristics and use them. They can then praise and reward the child for being helpful. Try to find something that the child can do that no one else in the family can. It might be taking things apart or calling the dog in because the child is the loudest member of the family.

Whenever possible give the child choices when there is work to be done. Studies on ADD children have shown that these children can be as focused as normal children when they are self-directed.. It is when they are directed by others to do things that they have trouble focusing on and finishing things. If parents give their child some choice in things, the child will be more successful in accomplishing a task. "Would you rather take out the garbage or set the table?"

As discussed before, we all need to find our area of expertise. ADD children tend to be creative and innovative; however, these abilities are often overlooked because of all of the negative characteristics exuded by ADD children. Parents should be on the lookout for abilities that the child comes by naturally. These could be athletics, art, music, storytelling, etc. If the adult can identify an ability, it should be encouraged so that the child can feel that he or she is an expert in this area. It's important for the parent to let the school know what their child's abilities are so they can be used in the classroom.

Mentor

One thing that is often overlooked in trying to help a child build self-esteem is finding a significant adult to befriend the child. We can all remember adults who influenced us as we were growing up. ADD children especially need that special person. The person can be a relative, family friend, coach, Sunday school teacher or any person who can relate to the ADD child. The parent should always be on the lookout for that adult. The parent should encourage the relationship and let that special adult know how important he or she is to the child. That person can be a sounding board for the child and serve as an advisor who doesn't carry the burdens that a parent does.

Self-Talk

Children with low self-esteem often think the worst. They view failure as being something that is out of their control. It is usually someone else's fault when they meet with failure. People with positive self-esteem view failure as part of a learning experience and use positive self-talk to prepare for the future. They say things like, "I'll do better next time" or "I know how I can do better next time." ADD children can be taught to talk positively to themselves and this in turn will lead to more success.

Having positive self-esteem will help the ADD child deal with the many setbacks that will be experienced throughout life. Children who are down on themselves cannot learn either in school or from experience. Learning is a risk and requires the person to take a risk of failing. The child who is down on himself or herself will not be willing to risk and consequently will not learn. The ADD child who does not have positive self-esteem is at real risk of dropping out or acting out.

Hints:

- Children need to feel needed and that they can contribute.
- They need a sense of autonomy or power.
- They need to become expert in some area.
- They need to find a significant adult who will listen to them and guide them.
- They need to learn positive self-talk.
- They need to understand that failure can be viewed as one step closer to success.

Common Behavioral Problems

Social Skills

Many ADD children have poor social skills. Most children develop social skills by observing cause and effect. If you step on someone's toe, you notice that person is unhappy with you. You soon learn that if you say you are sorry you will be forgiven. ADD children, because of their inability to focus attention do not learn to read the social cues. If they get into a verbal fight with a parent, they do not notice that the parent's face is turning red and that his or her neck veins are distending. Consequently, they keep pushing until the parent explodes. The ADD child is in shock that the parent is so upset. The child often feels that he or she did nothing wrong. This inability to read social cues and modify one's own behavior leads to many problems for the ADD child.

The ADD child has enough problems to deal with and having poor social skills just makes dealing with all problems harder. The ADD child needs more support from adults and peers than other children. Poor social skills can lead to rejection by adults and peers making it hard to get the needed support. As a result, ADD children often feel sad and lonely. They frequently have no idea of how their behavior has contributed to the rejection they experience from others. They often search for any friend and end up finding only problem children to associate with.

Social nuances: One area of concern is poor awareness of social nuances when dealing with people. ADD children don't learn the customs of the group. They have trouble following group rules and consequently step on other children's toes and don't even realize it. They tend to be possessive of things and friends. They have difficulty sharing and are often jealous of others. Many ADD children tend to be bossy and argumentative. They interrupt conversations and don't keep appropriate space between themselves and others. None of these characteristics endear one with peers.

Self-centered: Their unawareness of their actions and their interpretation of things leads to difficulties with peers and adults. Many times the ADD child, because of being egocentric thinks the parents are being overly critical when they correct him/her. They frequently feel that it was someone else's fault and not their own when things go wrong. Some ADD children take things very literally and can't understand jokes or take being teased. It's okay to tease someone else but they can't tolerate being teased. This leads to becoming the scapegoat of the group.

Over aroused: Many ADD children have problems with being emotionally over aroused. They overdo everything. They cry easily and have quick tempers. At times they get over excited and ruin a pleasant time or event for everyone. This makes the ADD child appear younger and he or she often has problems with developing age-appropriate relationships.

Treatment

Most ADD children need to be taught social skills because they have not learned them. ADD children can learn what they are supposed to do in social situations but often do not apply that knowledge in the real world. Behavioral literature suggests that children can learn social skills but cannot learn to apply those skills in new situations. Some experts think that the key is to teach the social skills and then go a step further and teach the child how and when to use them. Most people feel it is worthwhile to work on skills and that it provides some benefit. The hope is that we will learn how to better teach the utilization of social skills.

We communicate with the world around us in two different ways. The first is called nonverbal communication and the second is verbal communication. Non-verbal communication involves personal space, body language and facial expressions. Children must be taught how close to get to people when talking, and to read whether the person is angry or happy. They must also learn the social skill of making eye contact when speaking and shaking hands.

Parents need to teach their children to notice other people's nonverbal cues. This can be done by watching movies and asking the child whether the character is angry, happy, or sad. Parents can do the same thing when they go to the shopping mall. The point is to get the child to start analyzing nonverbal cues and recognize their importance in dealing with the world that surrounds the child.

Hints:

- Discuss the importance of the proper skill and why it will help the child become more successful.
- Demonstrate how to do the skill.
- Ask the child to demonstrate the skill.
- Set up situations for the child to use the skill (movie or the shopping mall).
- Set up a cue to remind the child to use the skill in new situations (e.g., some sort of hand signal such as pointing at one's eye to remind the child to look at the person).
- Reward the child for improvement and success.
- Recruit others to work with the child on the same skill.

Verbal communication skills require much more time and effort to develop. There are so many options available that the child can become confused and overwhelmed. The best thing to do is to look at problem behaviors and brainstorm with the child. The child should look at what problems the behavior is causing and seek alternatives. Parents can role-play social situations so that the child can practice new ways of handling these in a controlled environment. The parents can ask friends and family to help in the role-playing and reinforcing of appropriate social skills.

The Kick Me Sign!

Some ADD children seem to be picked on all the time by their peers. These children seem to be wearing a sign that says, "Kick me!" Helping these children overcome this problem involves teaching them verbally how to handle a difficult social situation. The parent might go through the program below and role-play the steps with the ADD child:

- Why are you being teased? (Because they get a rise out of you!)
- Who is in control when you get angry? (The other person, because if the teaser apologizes and gives you a present your anger goes away. If the teaser continues to tease you, your anger increases).
- Do you want to outsmart the other person?

The steps:

- Try ignoring (it takes a lot of energy to tease someone, and if you don't get a reaction, it's not worth the effort).
- If ignoring doesn't work, smile.
- Say, "Thank you so much! That's a compliment coming from someone like you."
- Exit - no matter what the other person says. Chances are the teaser won't know whether you are being serious about what you said or not and won't understand what you mean. That puts the ADD child in charge rather than the teaser.
- Practice makes perfect. Go through the steps above with the child and have them role-play with the parent being the teaser.
- Praise the child for handling the practice situation.

Hitting – The Hitting Game

Many children under age five have difficulty learning to control anger. Some of these children are aggressive and hit other children or adults when they are upset. Other children kick, bite or pull hair. All these behaviors are socially unacceptable and must be stopped. Most of the time the behavior will stop with a simple "no" or a time-out (each time the child hits, he or she is put on a chair or in a room for five minutes). Some children are more persistent and require different consequences. Usually, spanking makes aggressive children more aggressive. Rather than correcting the behavior, it teaches them hitting is okay when one is angry.

I am not an advocate of corporal punishment, but I believe that the consequence of pain can be a motivator to change behavior if it is done in the right way. A child who puts a screwdriver into an electrical outlet usually does not repeat this behavior because of the shock associated with it. As noted above hitting or spanking a child when the adult is angry is not effective; however, the shock of getting a rap on the forearm from someone smiling can cause the child to re-evaluate what he or she is doing.

The hitting game is an attempt to use psychological and game playing techniques on the child. The idea is to change the game to one the parent wins no matter whether the child changes behavior or not. No one wants to play a game that results in a loss each time it is played. The parents win if the child stops the behavior, or if the child continues the behavior the parent will win the hitting game.

The hitting game takes place whenever a child hits or threatens to hit a parent or another child. The child is given a rap on the upper arm by the parent. The parent does the following with a smile:

- Gives the child a rap on the bone of the upper arm with his or her knuckle.
- Smiles at the child and asks, "Isn't that fun? Do you want to play the hitting game some more?"
- If the child says "yes," you give another rap a little harder until the child says "no."
- If the child strikes another child, you say, "That child doesn't want to play with you. I'll play with you." The parent plays the game as above.

- If the child says, "No, I don't want to play," the parent says, "I'm sorry, I thought you wanted to play." No rap required. The child has decided that this game is no longer fun.
- Keep smiling!

Children are not dummies. Once they learn that they can't win the game, they will stop playing. The parent is in control of the game and isn't using excessive force – just enough to make this game a little painful for the other player. No one continues to play a game when it hurts and when he or she loses every time.

For kicking and biting, the game is still called the hitting game. A rap on the forearm is still used because the parent can control the force of the rap better than a kick or bite. For hair pulling, a little tug on the child's hair does wonders in stopping a repetition of hair pulling. Remember, you need to keep smiling while playing this game in order for it to work!

If the above doesn't help after a few episodes, obtain psychological consultation.

Lying

Almost all children tell lies at some time during their childhood. Often our attempt to stop the lying actually makes it worse.

Why do children lie? The two main reasons for lying are: an attempt to cover up something they did wrong and to avoid something they don't want to do. " I did all my homework." They have also seen peers lie and get away with things. Children have heard adults tell friends, "Your new hairdo looks great!" After the friend leaves, they have heard the parent say to the spouse how bad the new style really looks. Another example of lying in today's society is when the phone salesperson calls up and you tell the kids to say that you are not home.

Children continue to lie because they have avoided punishment or work by doing so. Sometimes they continue to lie so that they can debate over whether they are lying rather than correcting the wrong or doing the work. Also, children soon learn that they get a lot of adult attention for the lying. If parents become upset about the lying, the child begins to control the adult. If the child apologizes we feel good and if the child declares that he or she is not lying, we go crazy!

Behavioral Problems

ADD children lie more often than other children. Their disorder results in criticism and accusations of wrongdoing. They become defensive and make up excuses for not being successful.

Concept: The double edged-sword. Make it cost more for the child to lie than not to lie. Reward the child when he or she accidentally tells the truth.

- If you know the child did something, don't ask the child, "Did you do it?" When you give the child a chance to lie - you have a 50/50 chance of being told a lie. If the child has jelly on his or her hand and jelly was spilled on the floor don't ask, "Did you spill the jelly?" Say, "Clean it up!" Thank the child for helping when the problem or chore is done.

- If the child doesn't argue or lie, help them clean it up. This makes it more worthwhile to tell the truth!

- If they say, "I didn't do it," you say, "I don't care if you did or didn't. Get it cleaned up and I have something else for you to do afterwards." This means that it costs more to tell a lie.

- If you don't know which one of the kids did it, they all help clean it up and get extra chores. This means that sibs will put pressure on the culprit to tell the truth next time.

- Suppose the wrong child has to clean up something that he or she didn't do. No big deal! We all make mistakes, but we will be right 90% of the time. We haven't accused the child of lying and we have thanked him or her for doing the chores.

- Catch the child telling the truth and express how proud you are of him or her for telling the truth. Set the child up to be truthful. When you know that the child has brushed his or her teeth ask, "Did you brush your teeth?" When the child answers "yes," say "That is great! You are always truthful."

- New attitude for parents: You don't care if the child lies - you can't lose. The child is going to learn an important lesson about honesty and you are going to get some free labor.

Hints:

- Don't give the child a chance to lie.

- If the child tells a whopper, smile knowingly and say, "okay but you still have to correct the problem and by the way I have some extra work for you to do."
- Keep smiling.

Encopresis or Soiling

Children who soil their pants have a complex problem. Physical, emotional, behavioral and other issues have to be considered.

The most common cause for soiling is chronic constipation. When the child is constipated and has a bowel movement, it hurts to pass the stool. Therefore, the child tries to keep from having a bowel movement because of the associated pain. The child learns to relax the abdominal muscles and tighten the rectal sphincter muscles. If this has gone on for several months, the colon gradually enlarges to hold the stool. A large hard mass of stool develops near the rectum and pushes the rectum partially open allowing soft stool to leak out the rectum and soil the pants.

The initial cause of the constipation is long forgotten. Why does it continue? There are many reasons why the soiling continues. The primary reason is that it hurts to pass a large hard bowel movement. Oftentimes the child also gets attention for these problems and has the power to drive parents crazy. The child must become responsible for the problem rather than the parent. The parent can help the child by making it the child's problem, by rewarding success, and by using natural consequences.

Treatment Program

- Physical exam to rule out a physical problem.
- Remove the pain.
- Draw a diagram to show that the child has a physical problem (large stool in the rectum).
- Mineral oil: Two tablespoons morning and evening.
- Suppositories or enemas as a last resort to get things going (only if the oil is not helping).

Bowel Retraining

Have the child sit on the toilet for five minutes after breakfast or dinner. Eating stimulates the intestines.

Reward Success

The child has to retrain muscles and this should be rewarded.

The parent and child should go out and buy six prizes.

- One of these is taped to the mirror in the bathroom.
- When the child has a bowel movement (BM) in the toilet, he or she gets the prize.
- One Prize/Day Allowed

Schedule:

- Prizes 1&2: One prize immediately for each bowel movement in the toilet.
- Prizes 3&4: One prize after two bowel movements in the toilet.
- Prizes 5&6: One prize after three bowel movements in the toilet.

Natural Consequences for Accidents

- If the child has an accident, he or she has to clean up the underwear.
- No punishment for accidents. Only success is given attention.

Long-Term Treatment

- Most children need to be on mineral oil for 3-6 months.
- If the child has been successful for 3 months, a different stool softener could be tried: Metamucil or Colace.
- Long-term use of mineral oil reduces absorption of vitamins. Give a vitamin supplement.
- For any relapses restart the mineral oil.

Enuresis

Enuresis or bedwetting occurs in 5% of five-year-old children. ADD children are no more likely to have enuresis than normal children. It is more common in boys than girls and if nothing is done one-half of the children will be dry by the next year. However, bedwetting does cause some problems and is another strike against the ADD child who has the problem. It is a nuisance to have to change the bedding nightly and some children won't go on a sleepover because of the fear of being embarrassed if they wet the bed. There is debate as to the cause of the disorder. Research has shown that most children who wet at night have a functionally small bladder, which means that they cannot hold as much urine as normal children. There is also a group of children who are very sound sleepers.

There is debate over treatment of the disorder. Most physicians feel that a urinalysis should be done to rule out diabetes or a urinary problem. All experts would agree that a physician should be seen to evaluate the child if there is daytime wetting or a history of urinary infections. These children require a more thorough evaluation. There are three treatment programs that have shown some success.

Behavior Techniques First

There are numerous behavioral techniques that have been used with children who have enuresis. The first is to make the child responsible for the problem. This means the child learns to change the wet bedding, wash the sheets and make the bed. This hopefully serves as an incentive to work on solving the bedwetting problem. Some behavioral programs have the child measure how much urine he or she can hold. The child is then asked to hold the urine for increasingly longer periods of time. The child is rewarded for holding larger amounts of urine.

The last behavioral method is an imaging and/or practicing technique. In this program, the parent has the child lie down and shut his or her eyes as if asleep. The parent then asks the child to pretend that he or she has to urinate. The child gets up, turns on the light, goes into the bathroom, tries to urinate, flushes the toilet, washes hands, turns off the light and goes back to bed. The idea is to practice the drill so that it is easier to do during the middle of the night. Many programs also have the parents suggest to the child at bedtime that he or she will stay dry all night. Some also have the parent give the child a back rub an hour or so after he or she has gone to sleep. This slightly alerts the child, and the parent again suggests that the child will stay dry and wake up and go to the bathroom. All behavioral programs give rewards for dry nights.

Alarms

The most successful program is an alarm system. A Velcro patch is sewn on several pairs of underwear. A small sensing device is attached to the Velcro on the underpants and an alarm device is placed on the wrist or attached to a T-shirt with Velcro. When the child wets, the alarm immediately sounds. Usually the child is conditioned in several weeks to wake up before wetting. The alarm is removed and often the child starts wetting again. Using it a second time usually brings a permanent end to the wetting.

Medications – Last choice

Any medication has potential side-effects and is costly. In general other methods should be tried before using medication for something the child usually outgrows with time.

Tofranil is an antidepressant that has been shown to help stop enuresis. Used in small doses it has few side-effects and helps about 30-50% of children to become dry at night. Its mechanism of action in helping enuresis is not known. Tofranil does alter the sleep cycle so that the child doesn't sleep as deeply. Some experts think this is how the medication helps enuresis. If dry each morning for a month, the child is slowly weaned off the medicine.

DDAVP is a potent hormone that is very expensive and is administered in a nasal spray. It is over 90% effective in stopping enuresis. However, once the medication is stopped the enuresis usually returns. Current guidelines suggest it should be used only for two months. Most pediatricians feel more data needs to be gathered on side-effects before it is used for extended periods of time. It is an excellent treatment to use for children going to camp or going on overnights with friends.

No - Treatment Option

As noted above, most children outgrow problems with enuresis. Many physicians will not treat children under age six with the above programs because they feel time has as good a chance of solving the problem as any intervention.

8

Dealing with the Adolescent

Joe was a fifteen-year-old ADD adolescent who was driving his father and mother crazy. He did okay academically in junior high but was not succeeding in high school. His grades had fallen to D's. He had let his hair grow long and was associating with the dropouts in his class. The parents had tried to talk with Joe but had been unsuccessful. He said all his parents did was criticize him. He started lying about his schoolwork and where he was spending his time.

Joe is an example of an ADD adolescent who is going downhill with the pressures of dealing with high school and other adolescent issues. With this state of affairs, Joe and his parents need help putting things back together. This will take time and energy along with professional help. Below are listed some suggestions that might prevent some adolescent problems from developing if they are followed during early adolescence.

Changes

Dealing with adolescent children is difficult at best. In ADD children, it can be overwhelming. Adolescence is a time of change. The child is developing physically, mentally and sexually. Academic expectations are increasing and the child is expected to produce more work and act like an adult. All these changes cause turmoil in the child's emotions. The adolescent is trying to become independent and make decisions on his or her own; however, the adolescent does not want the responsibility that goes with decision-making. This leads to many confrontations with parents and authority figures.

The adolescent is certain nothing bad is going to happen to him or her. There is a belief that dreams will come true and that he or she is invulnerable to consequences for his or her actions. This can lead to kamikaze-like behavior – especially in hyperactive-impulsive ADD adolescents.

The parents are going through changes too. They have been with their children for thirteen or more years and are entering a new phase of their own life. The marriage or job could be in transition. The adults are closing in on age forty. Their job is to begin to let go of the adolescent. However, this is not a simple task. They must loosen the strings slowly and realize that even the best of teenagers will blow some things. Hopefully, they have helped the child develop a positive self-esteem. This will make facing adolescence easier for both the child and the parent.

While it is important for the ADD child to have a positive self-image, it is also important for the parent to have a positive image of the child. Our expectations are often fulfilled; therefore, the parent must view the child in a positive way. All parents feel negatively about their children at times and this is more common during adolescence because of the adolescent's challenging attitude towards parental authority. If the parent doesn't like the child or can't picture having fun with the child, then the parent and adolescent need some counseling to try to resolve the negative feelings.

- What's the picture?
- Do you like the child?
- Can you picture fun or is there constant tension?

Ideas for Parents:

- Remember that the ADD teenager's negative behavior is result of complex issues as noted above. There is no one simple solution. ADD adolescent children also experience more frustration than average teenagers, which makes things more complicated.
- Pick your fights. ADD children have many faults and adolescent ADD children can be unbearable at times. The parent could be on the child's back all the time. If the parent is always negative, the child often gives up and doesn't try to improve because of the

feeling that he or she will be criticized anyway. It is better to overlook minor things and pick the big things to work on. Occasionally let the adolescent win some points.

- Set aside time to resolve conflicts. A trip in the car is a good time to discuss tough issues. Let the teenager drive if he or she is old enough. This gives the teenager some control over the situation. It also means you won't be interrupted. During these conversations always find something positive about the teenager to discuss before discussing problem areas. Talk about feelings rather than criticize. For example, say, "It makes me feel angry when you say those things. Is that what you wanted?"

- Discuss current events twice a week. Whenever the family is together spend some time discussing things that are happening in the news. Discuss what the teenager would do in similar situations. Or what does the teenager think the parents would do? If the teenager expresses values that are in agreement with the parent's, the parent should reinforce the value with praise for the idea. Many issues that the teenager must face are on the news daily (gangs, drugs, sex, etc.). Take time to discuss these issues as a family before the teenager must confront them.

- The teenager is use to being criticized and often doesn't listen to adult lectures. But the child may tune in if parents discuss themselves and their experiences. This will often open communication and allow the teenager to join in without feeling put upon by the adult. In working on communication, one trap to avoid is the question, "How did school go today?" The teenager often feels this is a setup for a lecture on how to do better in school or other areas where the adolescent could improve.

- Try to get to know your teenager. This is a difficult task. Teenagers don't like to discuss things with adults.

- Spend some quality time with the adolescent at least twice a month. Find something both you and the adolescent enjoy doing and take the time to do it. Avoid sensitive issues during this time. Enjoy it.

- Make your house a place where the teenager's friends can hang out. By doing this you will get to know whom the teenager is hanging out with.

- If the adolescent is not involved in anything at school or outside of school, encourage a job search. A job where the adolescent can be successful helps build self-esteem.
- Make it worthwhile for the teen to be truthful. Teenagers often lie when they are in pain. It is an attempt to avoid pain. If homework is painful for the adolescent, he or she will conveniently forget that there are assignments to be done. The parents' job is to set up situations where the ADD child finds it more worthwhile to tell the truth than to lie. See the chapter on behavioral management.
- Most importantly, get help if things are not going well. See the chapter on recruiting a team. Many times the parents can't see the forest for the trees within their own family. This is when an outside counselor or psychologist can help re-establish communications between the adolescent and parent. Don't be afraid to ask for help raising an ADD adolescent. The task is difficult at best.

Hints:

- Pick your fights. You can't win every argument.
- Resolving conflicts takes time.
- Discussing current events helps build values.
- Communication: discuss yourself rather than asking, "How are you doing?"
- Get help if things are not going well.

9

School —— What the Parent Needs to Know

Education

A good education is key to success in adulthood. For the ADD child to become successful, this must be a year-round project. Our brain's memory is like a container with a sieve at the bottom of it. To keep the level of information in the container from dropping, new information must be constantly added because some is always sifting out through the bottom. If we stop education for the summer, the child will lose knowledge and will start the new school year behind where he or she was the previous spring. If we continue education during the summer, the child will start school in the fall ahead of where he or she was in the spring.

Because of the ADD child's problems with focusing attention, it is harder to direct information into the memory. The opening to the ADD child's memory container is narrow. Information has to be carefully poured into the opening or some of it will miss the container completely and never be registered. This is why many ADD children learn better in small groups or with tutors because the child's attention can be better focused and the information directed into the container.

About 40% of ADD children have some sort of learning disability in addition to their ADD problems. This means that the holes in the memory sieve are large and more information is lost. Large amounts of information have to keep flowing into the container to keep the level steady. These children require constant repetition of information to keep from losing it. Consequently, ADD children need to spend more time on learning than other children. This means working after school, weekends and over the summer just to keep even.

Dealing with the School

School is the worst place for the ADD child to be. It brings to the forefront all of his or her deficiencies. The child is asked to sit down, shut up, pay attention, and produce written work. All these tasks are difficult for the ADD child.

Parents must become advocates for their child because they are the only ones with a vested interest in seeing their child succeed. Sometimes they must squeak and make noise to get appropriate help. Parents can help improve the school environment by doing the following:

- Parents must keep in close contact with the school and teacher to make sure the child is progressing. Don't wait until the end of the first marking period to see how things are going! Make a visit to the school before school starts and set up an action plan for your child with the teacher.

- The parent must help the school find some way to make the ADD child part of the school. The ADD child who feels needed will do better at school. This is not an easy task for the parent or school to fulfill. The ADD child can have educational, behavioral, and social problems making him/her feel unwanted. The school needs to find something that makes the child important to the school. Ideas may vary from sports, art, music, crossing guard, messenger, blackboard eraser, etc.

- Let the teacher know that you are willing to help out.

- It is a good idea for the parents to meet in the spring of the year with the principal and this year's teacher to plan for the next school year. Not all teachers can handle an active, impulsive, and distractible child. If the principal understands the problems and the needs, he or she is more likely to make the best choice of teachers. Schools are loath to change teachers after school has started, otherwise everyone would want a change at the slightest problem.

- Try to find teachers who are motivators for the child. Remember that the ADD child needs to be more motivated than other children to succeed in school because this handicap makes school difficult.
- If the child is having problems, you must problem-solve with the teacher and child and find solutions quickly. The longer you wait the more likely the child will become frustrated and get further behind.
- Recruit other team members to help the child, such as a school social worker, to work on peer relations and self-esteem issues if needed. See chapter on recruiting the team.

Conflicts with the School

Most schools try very hard to help all children. Some schools still find it hard to make accommodations for special needs students because of lack of funding or understanding of the problems. Parents have rights under federal laws that can be used to get help for children who are being ignored or have fallen through the cracks.

The Law

The federal government has several laws that protect children with handicaps. ADD children can qualify for special help under two federal provisions. These laws are periodically up for review and could change.

Part B of the Individuals with Disabilities Education Act (IDEA)

IDEA requires that all eligible students receive a free appropriate public education including special education and related services which are necessary for a child to benefit from education. In 1991 the Department of Education took the position that ADD did not need to be added as a separate disability category in the statutory definition since children with ADD who require special education and related services can meet the eligibility criteria under the category of "Other Health Impaired"(OHI). IDEA was reviewed and reauthorized in 1997 by Congress. The final regulations for implementing IDEA 1997 were published in March of 1999. ADD and ADHD were specifically added to the list of conditions which would render a child eligible for special education services under OHI.

Part B of IDEA guarantees the following:

- Free and appropriate public education to all eligible children with disabilities.
- Requires a full and individual evaluation of the child's educational needs.
- A multidisciplinary team must conduct the evaluation.
- Evaluations must be made without undue delay.
- An Individual Education Plan (IEP) needs to be formulated if child qualifies.
- Child can qualify if he or she has another qualifying disability (e.g., a learning disability).
- If parents disagree with the school, they may request a due process hearing.

Section 504 of the Rehabilitation Act Of 1973

This act prohibits discrimination on the basis of handicap by recipients of Federal funds.

"Handicapped person" is defined in the Section 504 regulation as any person who has a physical or mental impairment which substantially limits a major life activity (e.g., learning). Thus, depending on the severity of the condition, a child with ADD may fit within that definition. The law provides that the school:

- Must make an individualized determination of the child's educational needs for regular or special education or related aids and services.
- The child's education must be provided in the regular education classroom unless it is demonstrated that education in the regular environment with the use of supplementary aids and services cannot be achieved satisfactorily.

Staffings

After the school has evaluated the child, a staffing will be held to discuss the findings and to make an individual treatment plan. These staffings are often times overwhelming to parents. The parents are confronted with a team of professionals who talk in a foreign language. The parents usually do not have a good understanding of their rights. The following are recommendations that could help the parent survive a staffing:

- Review the testing results with someone who can explain their meaning before the staffing.
- Take someone with you to the staffing. Never go to a staffing by yourself.
- If the discussion becomes negative, ask the professionals what are the child's good points and how can they be integrated into the educational plan.
- Have older children attend the staffings. Discuss ahead of time the terminology with them so they can understand what is going on. Have them write down one or two points to include in their individual education plan (IEP).

Working with Teachers

The teacher is one of the keys to a successful education. As noted previously, many problems can be prevented if the right teacher is found for the ADD child. That is why it is important to find out who the good teachers are and request one of them for your child. The school will tell you that a parent cannot request a specific teacher. In reality the principal will listen to a parent's request and, if it is reasonable, will try to satisfy it. If you don't ask, your odds of getting the right teacher drop considerably.

As noted above, the parent needs to offer the teacher help. This can take the form of being a room mother or volunteering for special projects for the class. The parent should give the teacher information on ADD and suggest strategies that have been successful in the classroom previously. If the parents have tried several times to make such suggestions but the teacher has not responded, they should give up. Trying to force the teacher to do something that he or she is uncomfortable with is a no-win situation. Devote energy to working on other solutions for the problems.

Personality Conflicts

If the child and teacher have a personality conflict, discuss this with the teacher and see if things can be worked out. No one person can get along with everyone. If the conflict cannot be resolved, meet with the principal and provide examples of the problems. Ask that the child be transferred. Usually, the principal will suggest other solutions before considering a transfer. Go along with these suggestions but set a time for a meeting to evaluate whether the suggestions are solving the problems. Make records of these meetings and send the principal a copy of the notes. If the principal's suggestions are not successful, ask for a transfer again. This request will be either granted or denied. If denied and the situation is detrimental to the child, ask for a due process hearing or consider placing the child in another school.

Other Strategies to Help the Child Deal with School

Tutoring

Almost all ADD children benefit from tutoring. ADD children often learn more in an hour of one-on-one instruction than in eight hours in a classroom. Schools often say that a child doesn't need a tutor. This is because they might be obligated to provide the tutor if they suggest it. If the child is behind in an academic area, tutoring is needed to prevent the child from falling farther behind.

Learn to Use a Computer

Every child in today's society needs to learn how to use a computer. Those children who are computer literate will earn more money than those who are not. It is critical for ADD children to learn to use the computer. This is because a computer can help the child become more successful academically. Computers can help make the child's written work legible, and it can check work for spelling and grammar errors. Many ADD children don't have the patience to rewrite reports – computers make this process much less labor intensive. Computer programs can motivate a child to work on weak areas and to work on repetitive tasks like math facts.

The child needs to take a keyboarding class or learn to type with one of the keyboarding programs that can be purchased (Type Tutor, Mavis Beacon Teaches Typing, and Mario Brothers Typing). Once the child can type twenty words per minute, typing becomes more efficient than writing by hand.

Homework

Homework is probably one of the most frustrating events in the life of parents and their ADD children. It requires organization and attention to detail. Students have to write down assignments and bring home the right books. The ADD child has to be motivated to work on something that is time consuming and difficult. If the child rushes through it, it will not be acceptable. Finally, the child must get it back to school and turned in without losing it. This is like asking someone to bang his head against a brick wall for six hours a day and then say that he didn't do a good job and therefore, must go home and practice the task for several more hours.

- As noted in an earlier chapter on prevention, start preparing the child for homework early by having a homework time in kindergarten.
- For most children it is better to do homework before dinner. Take a short break after getting home from school and then start working before the child gets tired.
- Have a regular time and place to do homework. This gets the child in the groove.
- The child may try earplugs, a fan or even soft music to see if this helps prevent distraction by the usual household and outside noises.
- Initially, parents might need to sit with the child to help with getting started and also with finishing the task.
- The parent should check the work for correctness, neatness and completeness.
- After awhile, parents should put more and more responsibility on the child. They need to back out of helping all the time.
- Ask the school to start a homework hotline or have a friend to call for assignments.
- Ask the school for two sets of books. It is better to get the work done than to fight about bringing books home.

- Use an assignment sheet or notebook. If necessary, have the teacher sign it.
- Trapper keepers (a large notebook with colored dividers) can help the child organize work to be done. A homework folder can also be used to get assignments back and forth to school.
- Study skills classes for middle school students are mandatory. These are classes taught by the school district or sometimes community colleges that teach children how to study efficiently and how to take notes.
- Motivate the child to find his or her own solutions.

No Homework—Great! Use the Win-Win Approach

Homework can be a painful experience for the ADD child because of problems with organization and attention. It is very tempting for children to say that they don't have any homework and thereby try to avoid the ordeal. Homework is certainly a low priority for the ADD child.

My favorite solution for dealing with homework avoidance is to tell the children that I hope they don't have any homework because I have something better for them to do. I tell them that I think homework is dumb and that I have a better educational activity for them to do. The activity is copying several pages from the encyclopedia. This is a great learning experience and the child gets to choose the topic! The child will be learning and working on writing skills.

Most children quickly decide that it is easier to bring homework home than have to copy from the encyclopedia. They are told they will do this activity even if there truly is no homework! The creative ADD students start making up assignments or working ahead, something that had never happened when the child was constantly reminded to bring things home.

You can't lose either way. If the child knows that he or she is going to have to do an hour of school-type work each night, there is little reason not to bring the homework home. He or she can't even get the parents aggravated because they are going to be excited about him/her doing the homework or copying the encyclopedia. The parents are now in a can't lose situation. As with all behavioral strategies, the key is to make it more worthwhile for the child to do the right thing rather than the wrong thing. The child then will look for a way to solve the organizational problem of doing homework. Probably, the motivated ADD child's solution will be better than the one the parent or teacher suggested.

Getting Ready for School in the Morning

Every school morning it was the same old thing. Jeff was always late for the school bus and the morning started off badly for everyone in the house. Mrs. Smith started trying to get Jeff out of bed two hours before he had to leave for the bus. After many reminders, he would make it out of bed about an hour before the bus came. He then went downstairs and ate breakfast in front of the TV. His parents had to practically drag him to his room to get dressed. It seemed the harder they pushed him to get ready for school the slower he moved. He became oppositional and his parents became frustrated.

Jeff is an ADD child who finds it difficult to get going in the morning and to get organized. It was noted that he had no problem getting up on Saturday mornings for basketball practice. School was a non-fun place to go to. The same old key works. Make it worthwhile for the child to get ready for school and he or she will. The following ideas are 95% effective in getting the child going without reminding:

- Tell the child that you are going to remind him or her once to get up in the a.m.
- That the child will need to have all chores done before watching TV or eating breakfast.
- If not ready fifteen minutes before time for the bus, the child will miss breakfast.
- That you are sure he or she can get ready and have breakfast.

Most kids will miss breakfast the first morning this consequence is put in place. It is amazing how upset they will be – even the ones who don't eat much breakfast. Some will go crying out the door saying that their teacher told them that they couldn't learn if they didn't have a good breakfast. Children are good at laying guilt on their parents.

- You tell them that there is no problem and you are sure that they will be successful tomorrow.

- Usually the second day the child gets up and ready without the usual struggle. The parents should say they knew the child could do it.

It's amazing how much better everyone's day goes without having to face an early morning battle every school day.

Hints:

- Use The Educational Calendar – education must be a year-round activity.
- Practice makes perfect!

The Educational Calendar

- August - Meet with the teacher before school starts. Start medication if the student has been off of it during the summer.
- Student should to do one-half to one hour of educational work every school night even if there is no assigned homework from the school.
- September - Start tutoring in weak areas.
- October - Meet with the teacher to see how things are going.
- Monthly - Phone calls with the teacher.
- January - Meet with teacher to look at ways to improve the next semester.
- April-May - Meet with the principal and teacher to plan for next year.
- May - Ask the teacher for suggestions for a summer educational program.
- Summer - Work daily on reading, writing and math. Find an activity for the child to be involved in that will build self-esteem.

Example 504 Plan

Checklist to be used at school for ADD children

Circle appropriate strategies:

Environmental Considerations

- Seating near the teacher
- Sit near a positive role model
- Study carrel to limit distractions when working independently
- Two seats to move between
- Seat away from distractions (high traffic areas)
- Ear plugs for independent work

Presenting Lessons

- Multi-sensory approach (support oral instructions with handouts, overheads, movies, etc.)
- Partner to check work
- Peer note-taker or tape recorder
- Use computer assistance whenever possible (math drills and written reports)
- Allow extra time if needed to finish tests and written work
- Allow extra credit
- Allow alternatives to written reports
- Assignment notebook (to be signed by teacher and parent, if needed)
- Help the child with organization (desk map, trapper keeper notebook, or colored folders for homework or by subject)
- Allow breaks and time to get up and move around

Behavioral Recommendations

- Classroom rules clear and simple
- Behavior contracting with the student

- Use the social worker to work on a behavior management system
- Use the social worker to work on peer relations
- Praise appropriate behavior
- Ignore inappropriate behaviors (as much as possible)
- Give privileges for appropriate or good behavior
- Remove privileges for inappropriate behavior
- Work with the parents on both behavior and schoolwork

Test Taking

- Untimed test
- Take tests in a resource room
- Try reading tests to the student and allow oral answers

Be Creative in Involving People to Help the ADD Student

- Guidance office: find mentor for the student
- School nurse: help child with medicine issues
- Psychologist: testing if needed and behavioral strategies
- Social worker: social skills training
- Enlist community agencies and volunteers to:
    - Develop after-school study programs
    - Develop after-school day care programs
    - Develop parenting classes
- Bus driver: train on behavior management and strategies for managing the bus
- Enlist parent volunteers for the classroom

Contact your local CHADD or LDA (Learning Disability Association) support group for more information on dealing with schools.

10

Behavioral and Educational Strategies —— School

General Behavioral Strategies

"To help Wade complete his work, we have tried reducing assignments, use of a timer and a reward, assignment sheets, and other various behavior modification systems. I know his parents have tried rewards and taking away privileges. Even with all this effort, Wade cannot get his work done. What else can be done to help him?"

The regular classroom teacher is having to deal with more problem children than ever before because of increasing budget cuts in special education programs. More learning disabled and behavioral disordered children are being mainstreamed into the regular classroom. When several ADD children are added to the classroom, the teacher is often overwhelmed with the task. In order for the teacher to survive, he or she must become an expert in discipline and motivation.

The ADD child with hyperactivity presents many problems for the teacher. One of the main problems is that behavioral techniques do not work as well for these children as they do for normal children. These children act before thinking because of their impulsiveness. The ability to think about the consequences of one's behavior is the cornerstone of all behavioral management programs. Even though behavioral programs are less successful and harder to implement with ADD children, they should be part of every program.

The next section outlines some general behavioral techniques for the classroom. These suggestions can be shared with teachers. There is not enough space in this book to go into great detail about classroom management.

Motivation

Motivation is the key to success in the classroom for the ADD child. As noted before, school magnifies the handicap. The ADD child has to work harder than other children to be successful. Make each child special and welcome in the classroom. Below are some ideas that successful teachers have implemented at the elementary school level:

- Each morning the teacher shakes each child's hand as he or she comes in the door and says, "Hello, I'm glad to have you in the class today." This starts the class out in a positive way and works on social skills at the same time.
- During the first week of school, call or talk with each child's parent. Ask about the child's strengths and weaknesses. Ask if the parent has suggestions – this recruits the parent to the team.
- Ask the parent to review schoolwork and read with the child on a daily basis.
- Make a card file on each child with things like birthdays, pets' names, favorite things, etc. This means you know special things about the child and can use them if the child needs to be motivated. "Write about Michael Jordan your favorite basketball player."
- Make the child feel needed especially those who are struggling academically. Find out if the child has any special talents and try to use those talents in the classroom. If there no any special talents, have the child become a helper (e.g., water the plants, erase the blackboard, etc.)
- Set up situations where the child can be successful.

Self-Esteem

The child who has good self-esteem will do well in the game called life.

- Find something positive to say about each child. The rule is two positives for every correction. With ADD children this is sometimes difficult to do, but it is amazing how effective it can be.

- Never belittle a child. Teachers and parents have to be careful about how they say things. Sometimes the adult is just teasing the child, but the child interprets it as a put-down.

Modifying Behavior – The Basics

The teacher needs to take an inventory of what can be used to modify behavior. These ideas usually are divided into two categories: one being motivators or rewards for appropriate behavior and the other being consequences for inappropriate behavior.

Rewards

- Edibles
- Privileges
- Parental given rewards
- Praise from teacher
- Approval from classmates
- Material rewards, stickers, etc.
- Earn time for a favorite activity

Consequences

- Spankings - can't be used!!
- Loss of privileges
- Homework
- Time-out in hall, in office, in room
- Peer pressure

Step One

Define the behavior that needs to be corrected. At first glance this would seem to be an easy task; however, not all behaviors can be corrected at once. The behaviors must be prioritized according to importance (i.e., the most disruptive behavior to the classroom). After the most troublesome behavior has been defined, an action plan can be instituted using the resources available to the teacher.

One further consideration needs to be evaluated before a plan is instituted. The classroom's primary objective is education and not behavioral management. Studies have shown that children learn more when educational objectives are set rather than when solely behavioral objectives are used. For example, if a child is overly active, the behavioral goal might be to have him or her sit quietly for five minutes while the educational goal of completing five work pages in a reasonable time might accomplish the same behavioral goal as well as accomplishing an educational goal.

Step Two

The teacher should try to determine what has worked previously for the child. This can be learned from observation in the classroom, talking with the ADD child's previous teacher, or talking with the ADD child's parent. For most ADD children, a simple positive stroke from the teacher might be enough of a reward. For the severe ADD child, it is very hard to find a workable approach that is beneficial to the child and rewarding to the teacher.

Professionals can come up with wonderful behavioral programs that are totally impractical for the individual classroom or the individual teacher. The teacher should decide how much time can be devoted to the individual child and what method best fits that time allowance. The teacher needs to decide which approach best fits his or her own personality.

Rewards: Rewards can be great motivators for children. As noted above, many ADD children will respond to positive verbal praise ("You did a good job") and nonverbal strokes (an approving smile). Please see the list of possible rewards. With more severe ADD children, the reward system often seems to work at first, but then the child gets bored with it and stops trying to work on the behavior, requiring the teacher constantly to change the reward and the method for giving rewards.

Consequences: Consequences for inappropriate behavior can be an effective method of establishing more appropriate behavior. The idea is to make it worthwhile for the child to do things right the first time, so it doesn't cost the child extra time later. See the list of consequences; (e.g., finish homework in school so you don't have any at home). Consequences presuppose that the child can focus attention on the behavior, is not overly impulsive and can think and weigh the consequences before acting. Obviously, many ADD children do not respond to consequences.

Cognitive training is being tried in an attempt to have the ADD children become more responsive to consequences of their behavior. The child is taught a strategy to think and analyze consequences before acting. Studies have shown that for most ADD children this has been of little benefit in helping them to control their behavior. However, the major problem has been that the child can learn to use the strategy in one situation but can't use this technique in new situations. More research needs to be done on how to teach children to generalize strategies to new situations. If this can be done, the cognitive training will be more effective.

Ignoring Minor Problems

Studies show that scolding a misbehaving child is closer in its behavioral effect to praising than to punishing. See chapter on "Teach" and the Win-Win Approach about reminding children and its detrimental effects on behavior. Teachers must learn to ignore minor behavioral problems and try to focus on positive behavior. Even minimal reprimands can be reinforcing to the ADD child who likes to have attention. Not only should reminders about behavior be as inconspicuous as possible but the teacher also needs to work with the whole class so that the ADD child does not get peer attention for inappropriate behavior.

Secret Signals

Many teachers have found that a secret signal, known only to the ADD child, can be an effective reminder. The teacher contracts with the ADD child to use a secret signal such as throat clearing or snapping fingers. Only the ADD child and the teacher know this signal. Upon hearing the signal, the child is to modify his or her behavior. The teacher can use this signal without looking at the child and after class, can reward the child. If the signal is not effective then the teacher can use some other contingency. This allows the teacher to focus on appropriate behavior and improvement in behavior and performance. There is little or no attention given to the undesirable behavior and improved behavior is rewarded with attention and praise. Children feel special when they have "secrets" that only they and the teacher share and this by itself sometimes improves behavior.

Assertive Discipline

Many schools are using assertive discipline procedures with children with excellent results. This method involves setting clear expectations for appropriate behavior, clear procedures for implementation of the program within the classroom, and clear consequences for inappropriate behavior. In most cases the teacher either writes the misbehaving child's name on the board or gives a ticket as a warning. When the child receives two or three tickets or check marks by his name he loses privileges or he is punished. This method is effective because it gives the child minimal attention for the problem behavior.

Contracts

Contracts can be made with individual ADD children to help them set clear goals for improvement. Contracts can deal with social or educational objectives and can involve just the teacher and the student or they can include social workers and parents. The child can earn rewards for accomplishing educational tasks or improving behavior. The child may suffer consequences for failing. Contracts are good for ADD children because they are written down and can be referred to on a regular basis. The idea that the child has agreed to something in writing and signed his or her name to it sometimes adds greater weight to the promise as compared to a verbal contract that can be debated later.

Emotions

Some children like to challenge the teacher's authority. Most people find it difficult to deal with a direct assault on their authority; however, if they can remember that a good teacher remains calm in the heat of battle they will have a better chance at winning the war.

When a teacher is provoked to anger, who is in control of the situation? It is obvious that the ADD child is in control. The child can give the teacher the "raspberries" and increase the teacher's anger or can say "I'm sorry and I won't do it again," thereby decreasing the teacher's anger. Teachers need to be calm and in control to help the ADD child. This is often easier said than done when dealing with a provocative child.

The Child Who Refuses to Obey

State the action that you wish to have the child do.

If the child refuses, restate what is to be done, set a time limit for it to be accomplished, and set a consequence. This statement should be made in a positive way with a positive expectation (e.g., "I expect that you will start your paper within the next minute or else you will have to go to the office"), as opposed to setting a negative expectation or arguing over who is going to make who do what.

Turn away from the child and make a positive comment to some other child.

If the child starts to do the expected action within the appropriate time limit, give a positive stroke to him or her.

Group or Class Rewards for Appropriate Behavior

The idea of class rewards is to make all the children in the class part of the same team. If everyone in the class gets their work done, the whole class receives a reward. Each individual in the class has a vested interest in making sure other members succeed. This is especially useful in having the class ignore attention-getting behavior of an ADD child.

Group rewards can be used in the same way as class rewards to help ADD children accomplish certain educational and behavioral objectives. With this technique, children are placed in groups and given assignments to accomplish. The groups can receive rewards for being done first or just for accomplishing the task. Sometimes this will not work if the ADD child has significant problems; the other children may not want the ADD child to be part of their group if they feel he or she will interfere with their success.

Token Economies

The basic idea of token economies is to reward appropriate behavior with tokens for each individual in the class whether that child has a problem or not. The tokens can be redeemed for privileges or material rewards. Many children respond with extra effort when they are rewarded in this way. Some teachers take tokens away for inappropriate behavior as well as dispense tokens for good behavior. All token economies have means of measuring the behavior and recording the earned tokens, a finite time for redeeming the tokens, and a maximum number of tokens that can be earned.

General Considerations

- **Motivation** - Behavioral control in an ADD child is a motivation problem. ADD children can control their behavior as well as anyone else if they are motivated. The problem is that it is harder and takes more energy for the ADD child to learn self-control. Therefore, the adult must learn motivation strategies to help the child become successful.
- **Expectation** - We must set positive expectations for the child. We must expect that the child can behave appropriately. If we don't set positive expectations, we are in trouble because children tend to live up to our expectations.
- **Ignoring** - When we are worn out and frustrated, it is very difficult to ignore a problem child's irritating behavior. But, it is important to try to ignore minor problems. Then we have more energy to expend on the bigger problems and the child has not developed a deaf ear from constantly hearing reprimands. If we focus on the few successes the child has, there will be a tendency in the child to try to get the positive attention rather than the negative reminding.
- **Discipline** - When discipline is necessary, try to do it in private and try not to give the child negative attention. Avoid demeaning comments and put-downs.
- **Goals** -Try to set educational goals rather than behavioral goals. If you want a child to stay seated, it is better to have the child do five math problems in five minutes than to have the child just sit still for five minutes. The child will need to sit still to get the math work done and the teacher will have succeeded with an educational objective as well as a behavioral one.
- **Payback** - Working on behavior management is difficult. The teacher is asked to try new skills and develop new strategies. Change is uncomfortable for anyone. When first trying a new method, it feels uncomfortable and awkward. The trick is not to make the change for one ADD child but to implement a system that will work for the ADD child as well as the average child. This will help the whole classroom work better. The eventual

payback will be less time spent on behavioral matters and more time available for teaching. The end result is that all the children will be more successful and the teacher will feel that he or she has accomplished the goal of helping children succeed.

Specific Educational Strategies

ADD children can be a strain on even the most patient teacher. It is important that each teacher know his or her own limits and work within them. The teacher should not be afraid to ask for help from other professionals within the school. It is hoped, that by using some of the suggestions outlined below, that the teacher will be able to circumvent or strengthen weak areas, thereby helping the child to become an asset to the class, rather than a liability.

The purpose of this section is to provide suggestions for management of specific ADD behaviors in the classroom. It is not meant to be all-inclusive and does not cover many basic educational strategies. As noted previously, ADD children have multiple handicaps that can be grouped into seven areas of weakness. The problem behaviors are concentration, impulsivity, inability to delay gratification, over arousal and hyperactivity, noncompliance, social problems, and organizational problems.

General

As noted in the first part of the chapter, all ADD children benefit from having a clearly defined structure in the classroom. There needs to be clear expectations, rules, and consequences.

Each child needs some individualization within the limits of the classroom. These will be outlined below.

Concentration

The ADD child's inability to focus attention is usually aggravated by the classroom setting. Most classrooms have many visual distractions (students moving in their seats, maps, pictures, blackboards, windows, clocks, etc.) There are also many auditory distractions (other students talking, the teacher leading a reading group, noise from the hall or outside).

ADD students have a hard time tuning out these multiple stimuli and concentrating on their work. The larger the number of children in the classroom the worse the problem is.

Recommendations:

- The child should be placed in the least distracting part of the classroom. This varies with each classroom. In general, the child should be away from areas that have traffic (doors, computers, and reference tables). He or she should not sit near the window. Seating near the teacher should be considered so that the child can be easily redirected when off task.
- The use of a timer can help the child focus on a specific project.
- Occasionally, ADD children need special modifications. Some ADD children benefit from wearing sound blocking earphones that were designed for industries with noise pollution. These are the children who are severely distracted by the noises of the regular classroom. Other children benefit from the use of study carrels where they are visually isolated from the classroom while doing seatwork. Both of these latter modifications should be tried only if the primary interventions have not worked because they single out the child as being different. Some ADD children do worse when isolated because there is no one readily available to redirect their activities.
- The child should be placed near students who will not provoke him or her.
- The child should be placed in small groups whenever possible; most ADD children are not able to function well in larger groups.
- The use of a secret signal is helpful to refocus the child's concentration.
- Older children can benefit from using a tape recorder for lecture classes that require good note taking skills or to record assignments.
- Use a multisensory approach to teaching as much as possible.

Impulsive Behavior

The impulsive behavior of ADD children can lead to many problems in the school. These children tend to act before they think. They start work before all the directions are given. This behavior can lead to spending time on the wrong project. They tend to rush through work making many careless errors. ADD children blurt out answers and talk out of turn. The latter problem can lead to social and behavioral problems.

Academic Recommendations

- Set academic goals for the child to achieve. "Answer the questions at the end of the chapter."
- Make directions simple and short. "Two steps."
- Ask the child to write down the steps that are necessary to accomplish the task.
- Use student helpers to make sure that everyone understands the work and how to accomplish it.
- Work on proofreading skills when the work is completed.
- Try using cognitive therapy techniques. Teach the child to "stop, look, and listen" before acting. A school social worker might be able to help in this effort.
- Use the Win-Win approach for impulsive behavior. Have the child copy a paragraph as a consequence for interrupting. Praise the child for copying or for controlling impulses.

Recommendations for Talking Out in the Classroom

See chapter 6 for an explanation of the Poop Scooper approach to behavior management.

- Positive - "I see you have lots of energy today! Thanks for volunteering for extra work by talking out."
- Obligation and Opportunity - "I feel obligated to give you an opportunity to use that energy. Please make me a copy of the reading assignment." The child can't interrupt while doing a specific task, and handwriting or some other constructive assignment is being completed.
- Praise - Praise the child for not talking out during the copying and for doing the task.
- Smile - You can't lose!
- Consequences - If the child refuses, remove privileges.

- Obligation and Opportunity - You have fulfilled your obligation to provide the student with an opportunity to be successful.
- Praise the child for volunteering to do extra work and completing it.
- Expectations - Expect that the child will learn quickly that it is not cost effective to interrupt.
- Relax - You are spending less energy on behavior management and the children are learning.

Need for Immediate Gratification

Many ADD children find it difficult to postpone gratification. They need immediate rewards for accomplishing tasks. They tend to be insatiable and need increasingly greater rewards to motivate them. This tendency makes it hard for the teacher to use any consistent behavioral management or motivation system. The teacher must constantly change the rewards.

Recommendations

- Be creative and flexible in designing any reward system.
- Make assignments short and nonrepetitive if there is no academic gain in repetitions.
- Use computers to work on repetitive tasks such as math facts.
- Use computers for written work.

Over Arousal and Hyperactivity

The ADD child's excitability and hyperactivity in the classroom lead to disruptions. These children are up and out of their seats. When they do manage to stay in their seats they are fidgety and distracting to others. They become overly excited and out of control easily. These children need to acquire greater control and purposefulness of their actions.

Recommendations

- Set academic goals. "Finish the assignment."

- If the child is antsy while sitting but is doing the work, don't correct him.
- Allow the ADD child to get up and move around the room if having to sit is causing difficulty. Give the child a purposeful activity: erase the blackboard, feed the fish, run an errand, etc.
- Many times physical stretching exercises for the whole class helps the child.
- These children should be encouraged to be in activities that allow them to burn off energy: soccer, dance, and swimming.
- These children, when self-paced in their own activities, usually have little problem. However, under teacher-paced activities, the work needs to be very short with breaks or quiet work should alternate with active work.
- Where possible give the child a choice of activities. He or she will be more motivated to do the work if allowed to participate in deciding what to do.
- Some children can benefit from a special desk in the back of the room where they can do work while standing.
- The secret signal as discussed in the previous chapter can help the ADD child to gain control again.
- Give the child something quiet to twiddle with. This will reduce the temptation to tap a pencil on the desktop. A "squish ball" or allowing the child to doodle at times actually helps some children focus.
- Be careful to prepare the ADD child for stimulating activities that might lead to over arousal (e.g., parties, games, contest, etc.). Discuss what might happen during the activity and ask how he or she should behave.
- Be creative!

Noncompliance

The noncompliant child is very difficult for the teacher to manage. Please see the recommendations in the previous chapter and consult with the school psychologist or social worker if the problem is a severe one.

Social Imperceptiveness

As mentioned before, social skills training might be of some benefit but has not been found to be as successful as people thought it would be. It is important that children learn the rules of social behavior. Children usually learn these rules by observation and experimentation. ADD children have to be taught these rules because they have not paid attention to the consequences of their social behavior. Children must learn to be diplomatic and tactful in dealing with others. ADD children often fail to acquire these skills. They impulsively demand to be the center of attention and blurt out their feelings. This social imperceptiveness can lead to loss of friends and a feeling of isolation.

Recommendations for Social Problems

- Social skills training with a social worker.
- The teacher should model appropriate behavior making sure not to mock the inappropriate behavior of the ADD child.
- For severe problems the parent will need to find help outside the school.

Organizational Problems

Many ADD children have organizational problems in school. These problems result from many of the difficulties already cited. Accomplishing tasks in the classroom is a challenge for the ADD children. Their desks are disaster areas. They don't have the right supplies or can't find them. They lose assignment sheets, homework, and supplies. They have trouble getting started on projects because they have not learned how to organize work.

Recommendations:

The Desk:

- Help the child organize the desk.
- Sometimes a map of the desk is helpful so there is a standard place to keep each item.
- Several cigar-sized boxes with dividers can be used to hold supplies.
- Frequent cleaning of the desk is mandatory.

Homework:

- Assignment sheets are helpful.
- The use of one notebook to keep all work in is helpful for the forgetful child.
- Use of a specially designed trapper keeper is helpful. A trapper keeper is a large notebook with dividers in it and a place for assignment sheets. It usually has pockets in the front and back. The front pocket can become a consistent place to put things to bring home and the back pocket a place to put things to take back to school. The idea is for the child to have only one thing to remember. "Bring your trapper keeper home every night!"
- Use a calendar in the trapper keeper to visually organize long-range assignments.
- Some children benefit from using a calendar date-book instead of assignment sheets for recording homework.
- If trapper keepers are not allowed because of desk size, a homework folder is helpful.
- Consider having an extra set of textbooks at the child's home.
- Communication with the parents is a must. Either a weekly phone call or a note system is helpful.
- A buddy system could be set up to make sure the appropriate books and assignments are going home.
- Some children benefit from the use of a tape recorder to record assignments.
- Set up a homework hotline or a friend to call for assignments.
- One strategy that has helped children remember their assignments is to have the child's parent require the child to copy pages from an encyclopedia if he or she doesn't bring work home from school. The child has a choice of remembering his homework or doing a more painful educational task. This is a powerful motivator for the child to bring the assignments home and to become more organized. See chapter on "Teach" and the Win - Win Approach.

Schoolwork:

- The use of outlines to help the child know what is important.
- Use check-off lists to make the task easier.

- Many schools have study skills classes so that children learn how to study more efficiently. Organizational skills are usually included in these courses.
- Use computers or word processors to write reports.
- The teacher should suggest to the parent that the child study in a quiet place with few distractions. There should be no television and the child should use the same room and table to do all schoolwork. Occasionally the child can benefit from some low background noise such as a fan or soft music.

11

Associated Problems and Their Treatment

Because ADD children have problems with attention, organization, and impulsivity, they are prone to develop problems in other areas. This chapter will discuss some of the problems that ADD children have that are associated with having ADD but are not part of the core symptoms. The chapter will also provide a brief overview of treatment strategies.

Jack is an eleven-year-old student who was diagnosed as having ADD in second grade. He has been on medication for four years and he was doing well until this school year. This is his first year in junior high. He has had difficulty getting his books and papers to class. He also has had difficulty getting his homework done. He has served several detentions for talking in class. Recently, he has become mouthy to teachers and is refusing to do any homework. His parents have noticed that he is becoming more argumentative and disrespectful. He has begun to hang around with the wrong crowd.

Jack is an example of an ADD child who is becoming frustrated as the workload in school increases. It is not uncommon for smart ADD children to begin to have academic problems as they progress into junior high and high school. Many ADD children cannot keep up with the workload as it increases and they become increasingly frustrated. Frustrated children tend to act out or drop out. They can develop low self-esteem and depression. Other children compensate by becoming oppositional and defiant.

Depression

Almost all ADD children become depressed or have depressive behavior at some time or another. This is because they suffer from chronic lack of success. ADD children are constantly told to pay attention and work harder. It becomes very frustrating and depressing to fail even when you try hard. When a child becomes depressed, he or she develops mood changes. Frequently, the child will stop trying, cry easily and have changes in eating or sleeping patterns.

Treatment consists of removing the source of frustration (if it can be identified) and finding some things the child can be successful in. Counseling is often beneficial in helping the child find strategies to overcome his or her difficulties and to realize that things are not as bad as they seem. Sometimes changing the child's stimulant medication or adding an antidepressant can be beneficial.

Oppositional Behavior

Every time mom suggested that Bobby do his chores, he would argue with her. He would explain that he was busy and that it wasn't fair to put such great demands on him. There was always a reason why things couldn't be done. He would never ever just say, "Ok mom." Mom was very frustrated and burned out from dealing with Bobby. (I suggested to her that he was preparing himself for the legal field!)

Many ADD children display oppositional behavior. Some children are just argumentative while others become that way when they are tired or frustrated. Sometimes stimulant medication can cause or worsen argumentative behavior, especially when the stimulant medication is wearing off.

Treatment consists of analyzing the potential causes of the oppositional behavior along with appropriate consequences for the behavior and rewards for improving the behavior. First, make sure the child is getting enough sleep. If the child is frustrated with something, try to find a way to remove the frustration before worrying about the oppositional behavior. If the child is on medication, see if changing the dose or timing of medication is helpful.

Social Skills

It was always interesting to have Delbert visit the office. You never knew what he was going to say. He would come in and tell me that I had the same tie on that I had worn the last time he was in. When asked how he remembered the tie, he would tell me it was because he remembered the dirty spot on it. Many ADD children say what they are thinking regardless of the social consequences of their thoughts. "You are dumb or you are bald."

ADD children have trouble with making and maintaining relationships. This is because the ADD children don't think before they speak or act. They tend not to notice that their intrusive behaviors cause others pain and irritation. The ADD child wants to be the boss and can't stand losing. Needless to say, these qualities do not endear him/her to other playmates. ADD children often become overly revved (excited and wound up) and step on people's toes without realizing what they are doing.

The ADD child must learn about consequences for behavior. The parent can help with this learning process by pointing out the cause and effect of behavior at every opportunity. Children can attend social skill classes in school or outside of school. Parents need to reinforce the suggestions made in these programs on a daily basis. The parent can also set up situations where the child is more liable to be successful, like inviting over one friend at a time and to have some planned fun activities to do. This will insure that the ADD child can be successful. The parents need to point out situations where the ADD child is being successful socially and give him/her praise. If the child is having serious social problems, the parent needs to find a counselor to work with the child and the family.

Organizational Problems

Jim reminded his mother of the absent-minded professor. He was a bright child who did well on tests; however, he also got bad grades. This was because he could never remember to bring his books home or turn in homework. He constantly lost his books, jackets and money. No matter what his parents tried Jim remained totally disorganized.

Jim is an example of an ADD child that has organizational problems at both home and school. The major areas of concern at home are getting chores done and keeping the room picked up. At school the problem is to get homework home, done and returned to school.

The best strategy for dealing with organizational problems is to make it worthwhile for the ADD child to become organized. Along with trying to motivate the child, it helps to develop organizational strategies with the child. Try the following:

- Have regular times for meals, studying, and going to bed.
- Teach the child how to make lists of things to do.
- Work with calendars. Write down on the calendar reoccurring events like scouts, baseball, etc. Have the child cross off each day so that he or she learns the days of the week and when things happen.
- Reward the child for improving organization and point out the consequences of not being organized.
- See chapters on school for ideas about homework.

Aggressive Behavior

Jeremy was always aggressive. He constantly was in fights and purposefully tripped children as they walked by his desk.

Aggressive behavior in ADD children has been associated with long-term behavioral problems. Aggressive ADD children are more likely to have run-ins with the law and authority figures as they progress into adolescence. It is important to try and modify this type of behavior at an early age.

The first part of trying to treat aggressive behavior is to determine when the behavior occurs. Does it occur at home or at school? Is it during structured time or unstructured time? Does it occur when the child is being teased or does it occur all the time? Sometimes changing the circumstances where it usually occurs can stop the behavior.

Counseling also is helpful for the child. The counseling should focus on giving the child tools to use rather than fighting. The counselor needs to teach the child to verbalize his or her feelings. Role-playing situations where the child would ordinarily become aggressive are helpful. Medication can sometimes help aggressive behavior. See the chapter on medications.

Fear of New Situations

Some ADD children find change difficult to cope with and become very upset and fearful of new situations. These children can be helped if the adult prepares the child for changes. This is done by using routines. The child then knows what is going to happen next. If a change from the routine is going to take place, warning the child about the impending change can smooth the transition. Developing a reward system for handling new situations can motivate the child to try hard at dealing with the change.

Moodiness

Moodiness is usually caused by either boredom or frustration. The moodiness can be improved by trying to help the child deal with frustrating circumstances and rewarding non-moody behavior. If the child is moody, time-out can allow the child a quiet place to get himself/herself together. The child needs his or her rest so he or she is not overly tired. Occasionally, medications can help the child be more cheerful. Then the less moody behavior can be rewarded.

Sleep Problems

Sleep problems are frequent in ADD children. If children do not get regular rest and are tired, they have more problems with paying attention and are generally more irritable. It is, therefore, especially important to solve sleep problems in ADD children.

It is important to define what the sleep problem is. Some children can have trouble getting to sleep. While others have trouble staying asleep. Many children just want to stay up and not go to bed. Did the child have problems before starting stimulant medication or did it occur with the start of medication?

Treatment consists of having a consistent bedtime that is enforced. Behavioral rewards can be used if the child goes to bed and stays in his or her room all night. Consequences can be used if he or she gets up or argues about going to bed. One consequence that works well with most children is to have them go to bed earlier the next evening if they either argue or get up. Reading before going to bed is often helpful in relaxing the child and making sleep easier.

Benadryl, Tofranil or Clonidine are sometimes used to help sleep problems. If the child is on stimulant medications, changing the dose or timing of medication can help correct some sleep problems. See the chapter on medication.

Checklist for Treating Associated Problems

- Remove causes of frustration if possible.
- Make sure the child is getting enough rest.
- Find ways for the child to be successful.
- Reward improvement.
- Propose consequences for inappropriate behavior.
- Review medications to see if they are aggravating the problem or could help lessen the problem.
- Consider counseling if things aren't improving.

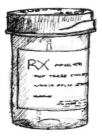

12

Medication

To obtain the maximum benefit from medication with the minimum of side-effects requires that all people working with ADD children have a thorough understanding of the medication. In the past, physicians prescribed medication with little or no follow-up. This is no longer an acceptable practice. Parents, educators, and physicians must communicate with each other. Each child has a unique response to medication. As with children who use insulin for diabetes, dosage and dosage schedules must be individualized for each child.

There has been a great deal of publicity recently about the use of medication in children with hyperactivity and attention deficit disorder. These articles suggest that medication is being used to "drug" children turning them into "zombies" who cannot learn. This adverse publicity has caused many parents to avoid the use of medication. This is unfortunate because medication can be an important aid in helping children with ADD. However, this publicity has been beneficial in that parents are now more aware of the potential side-effects of medication. As with any treatment modality, there is a potential for abuse.

Studies have shown that 70% of ADD children respond favorably to stimulant medication. For some of these children, medication is a miracle that allows them to begin to succeed at home and at school. For most children, medication is more effective in helping them focus attention than educational, psychological, or dietary interventions are. It is also quicker and cheaper.

While medication is the easiest and quickest way to help ADD children, there is always the remote possibility of serious side-effects. Therefore, other alternatives should be tried first. Long-term studies of medicated ADD children show that they can have significant social adjustment problems as they grow older. These studies suggest that using multiple therapies helps the children more than using just one therapy. There is no "quick fix" for this handicapping problem. Medication should not be used to help control behavior without working on the social, educational, and psychological aspects of the handicap.

Evaluation

The evaluation should include the following steps (see also the chapter on making a diagnosis):

- **History and Rating Scales:** A thorough history is the cornerstone in the evaluation of the child with ADD. The ANSER System (Aggregate Neurobehavioral Student Health and Educational Review) is a uniquely designed set of questionnaires to be filled out by the parents, the teacher, and the child (if over age 9). ADD behavioral checklists for teachers and parents are also used such as the Conners and ACTeRS.
- **Hearing and Vision:** Complete hearing and vision tests are mandatory. Children who have significant vision or hearing problems can act as if they have learning or behavioral problems. The ADD child with visual or hearing problems should have those problems corrected. Most children with ADD have problems with processing information they hear. This inability to tune into relevant material and tune out irrelevant material has been found to correlate well with the teachers' observations of classroom problems.
- **Physical and Neurological Exam:** A pediatric exam and neurological examination should be included to rule out any significant health or neurological problem.
- **IQ and Learning Disability Tests:** These are indicated if the child is having significant learning problems in school.
- **Laboratory Tests:** Brain wave tests (EEGs) to rule out seizures and specialized x-ray studies of the head (CAT scans) are not necessary in the workup of ADD children unless there are significant problems found on the physical examination or in the history.

The Brain and ADD

Research by Dr. Alan Zametkin from the National Institute of Mental Health showed that adult ADD patients have an abnormality in the way that their brains work. They perceive and process information differently than adults without ADD. See the chapter on Causes and Theory.

How The Brain Works

(Repeated from chapter on Causes and Theory.)

The brain works much like a computer. There are specialized areas that deal with what is seen and heard. There are other areas that allow storage of information and areas that allow the use of information to create new ideas. There are different areas that allow energies to be focused on one task at a time (the attention centers). These areas filter out nonrelevant material.

Imagine trying to watch TV, talk on the phone, and answer your children's questions while the stereo is blaring. Which stimulus is the most important and which stimuli are blocked out? Most people can respond to one stimulus and ignore the others. ADD children give equal time to all stimuli – touch, sound, vision, internal thoughts, and feelings. Their minds jump from one thing to the next. It is no wonder that these children are easily distracted, are unable to focus attention, are disorganized, are impulsive, and appear hyperactive. The inability to focus selective attention seems to be at the root of the problem.

Neurotransmitters

(Repeated from chapter on Causes and Theory.)

The attention center of the brain is turned off and on by chemicals. These chemicals are called neurotransmitters because they transmit information from one neuron to the next. Animal studies have suggested that injury to the attention center causes a decrease in neurotransmitters and is associated with ADD-like behavior in animals. Giving these research animals stimulant medication raises the level of neurotransmitters and allows the animals to function in a more normal way.

Neurotransmitters are formed from dietary proteins. Norepinephrine and dopamine are catecholamines that are synthesized in the nervous system from the amino acid tyrosine. Medications that affect the availability of these neurotransmitters to the central nervous system decrease ADD symptoms in ADD children.

ADD children are felt to have a lack of neurotransmitters in their attention centers. Anything that affects the level of these chemicals could interfere with the attention center and thereby cause ADD like symptoms. Diet and allergies can affect these chemicals in multiple ways and this might explain why a few ADD children are helped by changes in their diet. There are many more things that more directly affect the chemicals in the attention center.

Therapies For Treating ADD Children

Once a child has been diagnosed as having ADD, parents have to evaluate what options are available to help the child. Before starting medication, the parents should consider the following therapies.

- **Demystification:** Many children find ADD to be a mysterious condition. These children must learn what their unique problems are and what strategies can be used in managing the problems. It would be difficult to manage a handicap like diabetes if the child, parents, and physician did not understand the disease. Many times ADD children are labeled and no attempt is made to describe the problem.

- **Behavior Modification Techniques:** ADD children need individualized behavioral training. Behavioral training techniques are more difficult to implement in ADD children because of the children's inattention to consequences and because of their impulsiveness (acting before thinking).

- **Appropriate Classroom Placement:** These children benefit from being placed in smaller classroom settings and with teachers who can tolerate active children. ADD children should be seated in the least distracting part of the classroom, and in areas where it is easiest for the teacher to redirect their attention.

- **Expert:** ADD children often meet with failures in academic, social, and athletic ventures. This leads to a low self-image which in turn leads to less success. These children need to find some area in which they can become recognized as "experts" (being a little better or more knowledgeable than the average child).

Obtaining positive recognition from peers and adults can break the downward spiral that many ADD children experience.
- **Tutoring:** Many times ADD children can learn more in one hour of individual tutoring than in six hours of school. This is because the tutor can keep the child focused on work and there are fewer distractions when being tutored as compared to the regular classroom.
- **Counseling:** All ADD children and their families can benefit from counseling. Invariably, there are times when the children and their families need guidance on emotional, educational, and behavioral issues from an outside professional.
- **Support Groups:** Many parents of ADD children find support groups invaluable in helping them cope with the many problems that ADD children cause.
- **Trial of Medication:** Some professionals feel that all children with ADD should be tried on medication. If the child responds to the medication, they feel that the child should not be deprived of its benefit. They think that a good response to medication proves that the child has ADD. Others feel that medication should only be used after all other remedies have been exhausted.

Benefits of the Handicap

While there are multiple problems with having ADD, there are also some benefits. These children look at the world differently. They do not learn the same rules that govern most people's lives. Some ADD children, consequently, become very creative adults. Others, because of their energy levels, become very productive workers. ADD children seem to be on a different time schedule than the average child. They tend to function poorly in the morning, and they want to stay up later in the evening. These children can make excellent evening and night-shift workers as adults.

The school years are usually the most difficult for ADD children. The set rules and curriculum in school intensify all the deficiencies that ADD children have. Therefore, the goal of treatment should be to help ADD children survive in the school setting until they can find their own unique place in adulthood.

Stimulant Medication

ADD children and their parents need to understand that medication is not a "cure all" for attention problems. It is an aid in the total management of the problem. Using medication to help ADD children is similar to using glasses to help visually impaired children. The medicine helps the children focus. It does not make them smarter or make their behavior better. Children, whether wearing glasses or taking medication remain, responsible for their work and their behavior.

Stimulant medication has been found to be effective in over 70% of children with ADD. However, each child's response to medication is unique. Parents using medication should have a thorough understanding of the potential benefits and side-effects of the medication.

To Use Medication or Not, That Is the Question!

Deciding whether or not to use medication is a difficult decision for most parents. There is no easy way of knowing whether medication will cause more harm than good. There is always a worry about what the long-term effects of medication will be for the child. Looking at the potential benefits and risks for the individual child makes the decision somewhat easier.

Not a Cure-All

If medication helps an individual ADD child, there is a risk that it will be the only intervention used. **Studies have shown that medication can improve the behavior and attention, but it does not improve the long-term outcome unless it is coupled with other interventions already mentioned.**

Side-Effects of Stimulant Medication

Every medication is a potential poison. People working with ADD children should know what the side-effects of stimulant medication (Ritalin, Dexedrine, Dextrostat, Adderall and Cylert) are. If any of these side-effects develop, the physician can be notified and appropriate changes can be made.

Any medication can have a desirable effect or an undesirable one. For example, decongestants for colds can cause some people to be very sleepy. Other people become irritable and cranky. In some people, it actually is beneficial and helps to dry up the nose. Like decongestants, stimulant medicine can have either positive or negative effects.

Each of us is a different biological factory, and the same medication can react differently in each individual. The list of possible side-effects to stimulant medication is long and scary.

Seventy percent of children have no significant side-effects to medication and 30% have mild side-effects that dissipate with time. Less than 1% of children have serious side-effects that require stopping the medication.

- **Common Short-term Side-Effects:** For the first few days of treatment with stimulant medication, many children experience headaches, dizziness, dry mouth, constipation, stomach aches, sleep problems, emotional swings, and a "funny feeling." None of these side-effects are severe and they usually pass within a week. If the symptoms are severe or do not disappear within a short time, the physician should be notified so that adjustments can be made in the treatment program.

- **Loss of Appetite:** All of the stimulant medications can produce a decrease in appetite. Thin children seem to be more susceptible to this side effect than overweight children. Sometimes overweight children actually eat more on medication.

- **Decrease in Growth Velocity:** Some ADD children have a decrease in expected height at the end of one year on medication. This effect seems to be related to the dose of medication. Children receiving less than 0.8 mg/kg of Ritalin seem to experience little or no effect on height. Because of the possibility of both depressed appetite and the decrease in growth velocity, children need to have their weight and height monitored closely. This is especially true for children on large dosages of medication.

- **Insomnia:** Some children using stimulant medication have trouble getting to sleep at night. This is understandable because the medication is a stronger stimulant than coffee. Most children have no problems with getting to sleep or actually sleep better. Medication seems to help some children calm down so that they can relax and fall asleep faster. Sleeping patterns should be monitored closely because lack of sleep can aggravate ADD problems.

- **Heart Rate:** Stimulant medication increases the heart rate by five to ten beats per minute. It is not known whether this has any long-term side-effects.
- **"Zombie-like" State:** When started on medication some children become very lethargic and appear to be in a stupor. This effect usually subsides within one or two days and is equivalent to the sleepiness that some people experience when initially taking cold remedies. Other children continue to have problems. These children seem to be overly sensitive to medication and respond well to decreasing the medication. If this effect occurs, the physician should be notified and the dosage adjusted.

Serious Side-Effects - Contact the Physician

- **Allergies:** Medication should be stopped if the child develops a hive-like rash. This could represent an allergy to the medication and the physician should be contacted.
- **Precipitation of Tourette's Syndrome:** Tics and jerks. Stimulant medication should be used cautiously in children who have a family history of tic disorders. This is because medication can aggravate the tics. Tourette's Syndrome is an inherited disorder that causes serious problems. Initially, the syndrome can appear in childhood as an inability to focus attention. Over a period of years, the children develop tics, such as uncontrollable jerking of the face and shoulder. This is followed by verbal tics where children utter unusual sounds, such as grunts, barks or swearing.

  Most physicians feel that medication does not cause Tourette's Syndrome, but that it could lead to an earlier onset of symptoms in those children predisposed to the disorder. If any motor tics develop in children on medication, the physician should be notified so that medication can be adjusted or changed. In most cases, once the medicine is stopped the tics will disappear over a period of several months.

- **Dysphoria:** Some children who are placed on medication seem to have a significant mood change. They seem irritable, unhappy, and emotionally flat. If this persists, the child becomes depressed and has problems socially and educationally. Most of the time this condition is easily corrected by changing the stimulant medication or the dosage that is being used. Sometimes adding an antidepressant medication helps. The physician should be notified so that appropriate changes can be made.

- **Seizures:** Theoretically, stimulant medication could aggravate an existing seizure disorder by affecting the neurotransmitters. However, in clinical practice this has not been a problem. Many people have better control of their seizures once stimulant medication is started for their ADD problems.

Long-Term Effects

Stimulant medication has been used for ADD problems for over forty years. There have been no reports suggesting that there are long-term effects to this medication. However, with any medication there is the possibility that some detrimental effect will be discovered.

Associated Problems

- **Criminal Behavior:** Several magazine articles have implied that stimulant medication use could lead to criminal behavior (drug abuse and violence) at a later age. The few long-term studies that have been done in this area do not find this to be the case. Studies have shown that ADD children have more problems with the law and with drug abuse than do non-ADD children. Children who have been on medication seem to have fewer problems than the ADD children who have not been treated—but more problems than normal children. Interpretation of long-term studies is a difficult task. However, ADD children are at risk of becoming involved in criminal behavior because of their impulsiveness, inattentiveness, need for immediate gratification and low self-esteem. It is hoped that medication along with educational and psychological help will prevent the ADD child from becoming involved in criminal behavior.
- **Risk of Psychological Dependence:** The ADD child on medication may feel that the medication is keeping his behavior in control and that he cannot control his behavior without medication. Many ADD children call their medication "smart pills or good

pills." It is important for the child to understand that ADD is a handicap that makes it more difficult to focus attention and control behavior but that the child is ultimately responsible for his or her behavior off or on medication. The ADD child should not use the handicap as an excuse for poor behavior.

- **Drug Abuse:** There are several potential problems involving ADD children on medication. The first problem is whether these children are likely to abuse stimulant medication. Stimulants are used by some people in large doses to get a high. Studies have shown practically no abuse of stimulant medication among ADD children. This is probably the result of several factors. The first is that stimulant medication has a calming effect on ADD children rather than an euphoric high. The second factor is that no preteen or teenager wants to take medication that makes him or her different or is prescribed by an adult.

  Another potential problem is that the ADD child is learning to take drugs for all problems. Will the child then experiment with drugs when older? As noted previously, studies suggest that ADD children who take stimulant medication have fewer drug abuse problems than ADD children who are not treated. It is thought that ADD children who are treated with stimulant medication are more likely to succeed in school and feel better about themselves. If this is true, they are more likely to have a better self-image and are less likely to experiment with drugs.

  Recently, some children have been snorting crushed Ritalin and say that this gives the user a high. Studies have shown that snorting Ritalin causes a chemical irritation to the lining of the nose. Ritalin taken orally does not cause a high and the experts are not sure that it can cause a high by snorting. Some experts feel that the kids are really getting a rush from burning the lining of the nose. More studies will need to be done on this potential abuse of medication before it is known if this is a real problem or not.

- **Guilt:** Parents feel guilty about having a child with ADD problems. They feel they have in some way caused their child's ADD. Now they are going to give their child "mind altering" stimulant medication. They have heard on TV and radio that these medications can cause terrible side-effects. They are indeed in a no-win situation. If they don't give medication, their child will fail and if they do give medication there is a risk of side-effects and criticism from family, school, and friends.

Benefits of Stimulant Medication

There are many reasons to use medication. As noted many times before, 70% of ADD children have significant improvements on medication. Many children with ADD manifest some or all of the behaviors outlined below. The possible benefits of medication with each of these behaviors will be discussed.

- **Hyperactivity:** Hyperactivity is one of the behaviors that responds best to medication. If medication is effective, children will demonstrate less nonpurposeful activity. They will be able to sit quietly in their seats without disrupting the class. In the home, they will be able to better control their behavior as they engage in activities, such as watching TV and sitting through a meal.

- **Attention:** Another use for medication is to increase the ability to focus attention on work both in the home and at school. Medication can increase the ability to prioritize stimuli and to sort out the most relevant information. This leads to an increased ability to tune out distracting stimuli and to focus attention on work. In the classroom, there is an increased ability to produce work in a timely and efficient manner.

- **Social Skills:** Medication is associated with an increased ability to relate to peers and to become more socially perceptive. This change in behavior is related to an increased awareness of the environment, an increased ability to focus attention, process information and control impulsivity.

- **Noncompliance and Oppositional Behavior:** About one-third of ADD children have a tendency to purposely aggravate peers and adults. Unfortunately, studies show that medication does not decrease oppositional behavior. However, in a few individual cases less oppositional behavior is seen.

- **Impulsive Behavior and Inability to Delay Gratification:** Medication seems to decrease impulsive behavior. Children are better able to think things through before acting. They also seem to be able to wait their turn better.

- **Fine Motor Skills and Organizational Skills:** Another area of benefit is improved fine motor skills. Handwriting dramatically improves in about one-third of children. This is probably due to an increased ability to focus attention on the complicated task of writing. On medication, ADD children receive appropriate feedback from their senses and are better able to coordinate and organize the skill of writing. Many times other organizational skills also improve.

- **Emotional Over Arousal:** Stimulant medication often helps smooth the emotional ups and downs that ADD children experience.

Other Benefits

- **Learning Disability (LD) Problems:** Thirty to fifty percent of children with learning disabilities also have ADD. Medication makes the child more available to remediate the LD problem by improving attention and concentration. Studies have shown that children retain what they have learned while on medication and do not forget it when off medication. It does not cure the learning disability. LD children need specific educational planning and help.

- **Increases Success and Self-Esteem:** If medication helps the child in the above ways, the child will meet with increased success and he or she will feel better about himself or herself. Once the ADD child starts to succeed, the other interventions become more successful.

- **Stimulates the Brain:** Medication stimulates part of the brain that is not functioning well. Experiences from working with children with physical handicaps show the importance of stimulating nerves and nerve pathways. If a child has a partial paralysis of a limb and does not use it, the handicap does not improve. If the child works hard at rehabilitation, function will be improved. Many times the handicapped child can benefit from crutches or braces during this rehabilitation. Similarly, medicine can be used as an aid in the rehabilitation of the ADD child. It is to be hoped that medication will stimulate the attention centers so that they develop and eventually fire on their own.

Making a Decision?

The pros and cons of using medication have been outlined above. When academic, behavioral, and psychological interventions have been tried and the ADD child is still having significant problems, medication should be given a trial. In this case, the risks of medication usage are far less than the risks associated with chronic failure and lack of success.

In less severe cases where the ADD child has found some success with other interventions but is still having mild to moderate problems, the answer is less clear. Some experts feel that medication should be tried in these cases because of the possibility that the ADD child might do much better on medication than if it is not used. Others would argue that if the child is doing okay why risk using medication on the chance that the child might do better. There is no one answer to the above question and each case should be evaluated carefully. A decision can be made and then re-evaluated every several months. Many times the answer becomes apparent when following a child over time.

Using Medication

Using medication requires that teachers, counselors, parents and physicians work together. Medication is helpful in breaking the downward spiral of failure that ADD children experience. ADD children often have low self-esteem because of constant lack of success in school, at home and in social relationships. Medication helps the children focus attention allowing teachers, counselors, and parents to more effectively work with them. Without medication many children continue the downward spiral and may experience conflict with society and the law.

ADD children should be evaluated as outlined above and their behavior should be charted prior to starting medication. Problem behaviors should be defined. The time of day and the day of the week when these behaviors are at their worst should also be noted. Particular situations that trigger these behaviors should be recorded.

Once the behaviors are recorded, medication can be tried (see list of medications at the end of this chapter.) Stimulant medications are tried first because they have fewer side-effects and are usually more effective than other types of medication. The child is usually started on a low dosage, 0.3mg/kg/dose of Ritalin, and it is given once or twice a day. Medications are usually started on a weekend so that both child and parent can make sure there are no side-effects before the child goes to school. If stimulants are going to help the ADD child, the benefits are apparent within 1 hour of starting medication. The effects of stimulant medication last about 3-4 hours. Try to maintain the child on medication for 1 week even if the child develops some side-effects. As with cold medications, minor reactions can occur for the first several days when initiating medication. If major side-effects develop, call the physician. The dosage can be decreased or the medicine stopped.

After a week on medication, problem behaviors are again monitored. If there has been no improvement, the medication is increased weekly, monitoring behavior until the child improves or develops side-effects. If Ritalin has not been effective, another stimulant is used (Adderall, Dexedrine, or Dextrostat). Once significant improvement is noted, the child is maintained on that dosage.

Decisions on how often to give the medication are based on the behavior monitoring. Some children do well on one dose of medication a day. If these children start the day off on a positive note and are successful, they are capable of sustaining their positive behavior throughout the day. At the other extreme, are those children who can only function while on medication. These children often need 3-4 doses per day of the nontimed-release stimulants (Ritalin tablets, Dextrostat tablets, or Dexedrine tablets).

Medication should be used when medication is needed !

Some people are hesitant to give medication in the evening or on weekends. This decision should be made after reviewing the behavioral records. If the child is not having significant problems at these times, medication need not be used. If medication has been shown to be effective at other times and the child is having significant behavioral problems after school and on weekends, then he or she should not be deprived of the medication's benefit.

As noted before, some ADD children refer to medications as "smart pills." They feel that it is the medication that allows them to succeed and control their behavior. It is important to correct this idea and make sure that ADD children know that they are ultimately responsible for their own behavior. Giving medication on a regular schedule helps the ADD children feel that it is part of a daily routine. Telling a child that extra medicine is needed for baseball practice tonight makes the child think that it is the medicine that controls his behavior.

Using medication is like wearing glasses, it helps the child focus and see things more clearly. It is up to the child to respond to the information and make reasonable behavioral decisions.

Follow-Up

Children need to be followed very closely when starting medication. This requires the physician to monitor improvement and side-effects. Weekly contact with the parents and school are needed to help adjust medication. Questionnaires such as the Conners checklist and the ACTERS Scale help the physician monitor behavioral improvement. The physician should also monitor the child's height and weight along with the emotional reactions to using medication. The physician should be readily available to the parents, teachers, and others working with the ADD child.

Once the child has been stabilized on medication and the most effective dose has been determined, the child should be monitored by the physician 3-4 times a year. Children often develop a tolerance to the initial effective dosage, and their ability to focus attention worsens. This lack of effect is corrected by increasing the dosage slightly and is usually a one-time occurrence.

Guidelines for Starting Stimulant Medication

- Start on a weekend so that side-effects can be assessed prior to school.
- Start with a low dose and gradually increase. Adjustments can be made every 1-2 weeks until an effective dosage is reached. Start increased dosages on the weekend.
- If using slow release medication, give it once a day.
- If using short acting medication, give a dose in the morning and one at noon (coverage for the school day).
- If no significant problems arise over the weekend, continue medication for school on Monday.
- If problems develop, contact the physician.
- After 1-2 weeks contact the school to see how the child is doing.
- Call the physician after the medication has been used for several weeks so the dosage can be adjusted if needed.

- Make an appointment with the physician for a month after starting medication so that height, weight and blood pressure can be monitored.
- See the physician every 3-4 months so that progress and problems can be monitored and timing and dosage of medication can be optimized.

ADD Without Hyperactivity – *A Special Case*

In the past, children with attention problems and no hyperactivity have been neglected by physicians, educators, and psychologists. These ADD children have been classified as "daydreamers" or "poorly motivated." Sixty to seventy percent of these children are girls. Studies have shown that these ADD children tend to be very responsive to low doses of medication. See the chapter on ADHD and ADD Without Hyperactivity.

These children have few obvious symptoms. They are not disruptive and do not draw attention to their behavior. The following is a list of problem areas that these ADD children experience:

- **Organizational Problems:** They misplace and lose important things. Their desks are "disaster areas."
- **Daydreaming:** These children often seem to be in another world. What they are thinking about often has little to do with the task at hand. Their associations are frequently unusual. Their classmates may call them "air heads."
- **Distractibility:** These children find it difficult to focus on any task and are easily distracted by their senses and feelings.
- **Overly Talkative:** Many of the girls with this problem tend to "ramble on" when talking. They do not realize that they are annoying teachers, students, or parents.
- **Inability to Complete Tasks:** These children tend to be inefficient in completing tasks. They take three to four times as long as other children to accomplish a task. This problem can lead to poor school performance and to frustrations for parents, teachers, and children.

The best way of measuring these children's progress is to monitor their work output very closely. Many of these children take home large amounts of homework everyday. When started on medication, there is a decrease in the amount of homework. The parents will notice that the child is able to finish chores more rapidly. For example, they complete the dishes in fifteen minutes instead of the usual hour.

Medications for ADD without hyperactivity are the same as for ADD with hyperactivity.

Fine-Tuning Stimulant Medication

Tolerance

Children often develop a tolerance to the initial effective dosage and their ability to focus attention worsens. This effect usually occurs within several months of starting medication. This lack of effect is corrected by increasing the dosage slightly and is a one-time occurrence.

Long-Term Use

Some children seem to develop a tolerance to medication after they have been on it for a year or two. The effectiveness of the medication decreases even with increasing dosages. This is corrected by switching to a different stimulant.

When to Use Medication and When to Try Off

- Once a year children should be tried off medication. This should be done at a time of year that is calm – not during holiday periods when the child is likely to be excited.
- The best time to try the child off of medication is during the summer when there is less academic stress. It is important for the parents to pick a time when the child is in a routine and things are calm.
- The child should be tried off the medication for a period of one week and preferably for two weeks. Many times the ADD child takes a week or two to adjust to being off medication. This is because his body chemistry has to adjust to not having the

medication and he has to psychologically adjust to being totally responsible for his or her behavior.
- If the child is getting more negative strokes than positive ones, the medication should be restarted.
- If the child is doing well, the trial off of medication can be continued until school starts. Restart medication for school – see below:
  - **Summertime:** If the child's behavior is controllable, then the child can be taken off medication for the summer. If the child is being tutored or going to summer school, consideration should be given to using medication for those periods. If the child is having significant social or behavioral problems outside of school and medication has been effective in helping these problems, medication should probably be used during the summer vacation.
  - **Start of School:** It is important for the child to start the year out right at school. A good first impression of a student by the teacher helps the child be successful in the classroom. Therefore, medication is restarted the week before school starts in the fall so that the ADD child has a good start to the school year. If the child is doing well at school and did well off medication during the summer, he or she can be tried off during the school year. The best months for trying the child off medication are November or February because these months are usually quiet times at school and the child is in the groove of doing schoolwork.
  - **Weekends:** Oftentimes medication can be stopped on weekends or the dosage lowered. This is because the child doesn't have to concentrate as much at home as in school. Occasionally the ADD child will have side-effects each time medication is restarted (headaches, stomach aches, dizziness, etc.). These children have problems at school the first few days of the week until their bodies readjust to the medication. They can benefit from a low dose of medication on the weekends so there is no readjustment to medication on Mondays.
  - **Holidays:** In general holidays are an exciting time and ADD children have increased problems with controlling their

behavior; therefore, medication should be given as usual. The benefits of having a pleasant time as a family far outweigh the risks of a reaction to the medication.

- As noted previously, the goal is to get all children off medications.

Adjusting Medication

Is It Working? Generally there is little problem in knowing whether medication is working or not; there is usually a dramatic improvement in behavior. At times, improvement is harder to determine, or one observer says there is a tremendous improvement and another observer says the child is worse. This happens because medicine only works for 3-4 hours. If the child is taking a dose of medication at 8 a.m. and another at noon, the teacher might report that the child is doing well and the parent might report that the child is falling apart at home. Some children's behavior deteriorates so badly when medication is wearing off that the observer forgets that the child was pretty good for the first two hours of the medication. In these cases, behavior needs to be observed on an hourly basis to determine when the child is having problems. An extra dose of medication could be given or a longer acting medication could be tried to correct the problem. Obviously, if the ADD child's behavior is bad all the time then medication is not working.

Number of Doses

Some children metabolize or use up medication faster than others. The number of doses of medication given can vary from one to four doses.

Long Acting Medications: The use of long acting stimulant medication (Ritalin SR, Dexedrine Spansules, Adderall) can be considered when the regular medication is working for only 1-2 hours or when the child prefers not to take medication at school.

- Ritalin SR only comes in a 20 mg tablet. A few years ago it was thought that long acting Ritalin was less effective than the regular Ritalin. Newer controlled studies suggest that this is not true. We have found that the slow release is an effective medication but requires a slightly higher dose than the regular Ritalin.

- Dexedrine Spansules comes in several different size tablets and lasts 6-8 hrs.
- Adderall is a stimulant medication that lasts about 6-8 hours and is being tried once a day for school. For some children it seems to cause fewer emotional ups and down than Ritalin. It has the advantage of coming in several dosages and the tablets are scored so that they can be cut easily to adjust the dosage. It is relatively inexpensive.

How Long to Use?

Hopefully, as ADD children grow and mature, they will learn effective ways to deal with their handicap so that medicine will no longer be needed. Most ADD children require medication for 2-3 years. Seventy percent of children learn to compensate for their handicap and do not require medication into adulthood. Thirty percent continue to benefit from medication into adult life. The only way to tell if medication is still necessary is to periodically take children off medication to see if they are able to succeed without it.

Mood Problems

- **Depression:** Many ADD children develop depression at one time or another because of lack of success. Occasionally, medication makes these symptoms worse. Many times this problem can be corrected by changing the dosage of medication or switching to a different stimulant medication. If this does not work, adding an antidepressant, such as Tofranil, or one of the newer Selective Serotonin Release Inhibitors SSRI antidepressants, such as Prozac, helps the child's depression while the stimulant medication helps the child's attention.
- **Mood Swings:** Many ADD children have dramatic mood swings and dealing with these children can be like riding a roller coaster. Adding an antidepressant can smooth the ups and downs so that the child can function better.

Sleep Problems

As noted before, sleep problems can make ADD problems worse. If the child is not rested, he or she can be less attentive and more irritable. It is important to define what the problem is and how long it has been present. Does the child have problems going to bed, going to sleep or waking up in the night? Did these problems first occur when the child was placed on stimulant medication or did the child have problems before medication?

Stimulant medication can cause or aggravate sleep problems in two ways. In some cases the stimulant medication seems to cause a caffeine-like effect long after the behavioral benefits have subsided – the child is more alert. More often the ADD child experiences sleep problems because the mind races and is not focused after the medication has worn off. Often these children can calm down and get to sleep better if a small dose of stimulant medication is given in the late afternoon or early evening. It is our experience that this later dose will either help the sleep problem (about 50% of the time) or make it much worse.

Medication for Sleep Problems

- **Tricyclic Antidepressants:** (e.g., Tofranil) can be tried for sleep problems. The antidepressant helps the ADD child to relax and calm down thus making sleep easier. Antidepressants can also act together with the stimulant medication to help attention and they have the added advantage of making most ADD children less irritable. Frequently, the total dose of stimulant medication can be reduced when using the antidepressant in conjunction with the stimulant.
- **Clonidine:** A high blood pressure medication that has a side effect of tiredness. It is very effective in helping children go to sleep. Clonidine has also been shown to help aggressive behavior and hyperactivity.
- **Benadryl:** An antihistamine that is used for itching but is good as a mild sedative. It will help the child to get to sleep. The major problem is that most children build up a tolerance to the medication within a few days and the sleep problem returns.
- **Melatonin:** A naturally occurring hormone in the brain that is secreted during the sleep cycle. It is available over the counter at

most pharmacies and has been found to help some patients sleep better.

If the child is not sleeping well, it is important to solve the problem because lack of sleep aggravates all the ADD child's problems.

Age Related Problems

Many children under age five do not respond favorably to stimulant medication. It is felt that this is due to the immaturity of the nervous system. If these children continue to have ADD problems, medication can be of benefit at a later age.

Adolescents do not outgrow their attention problems. Their hyperactivity seems to subside as they get older and some learn to circumvent the other handicaps. Medication can still be a benefit to the teen if he or she is having significant problems. Usually adolescents need relatively smaller doses of medication per body weight. This is because of their slower metabolism compared to younger children. As noted previously, many adolescents prefer time-released medications so they do not have to take them at school.

Conclusion

As noted many times before, ADD is a handicap that requires multiple interventions. There is no one easy cure. There is no substitute for hard work. The parents, teachers, and physicians must form a team to help the ADD child reach his or her potential. Hopefully, this chapter will serve as a useful guide on the place of medication in the total treatment of ADD.

Medications – Stimulant

Ritalin

Ritalin (methylphenidate hydrochloride) has been studied more than any other medication ever developed. It is usually the drug of choice for ADD children. This is because we have more knowledge about it and we know within a day or two if it is working. The starting dose is usually 0.3mg/kg/dose. Serum levels can be monitored, but this is very expensive. Clinical observation is the most practical way to measure Ritalin's benefits and side-effects. Many states have laws requiring a handwritten prescription that must be filled within 7 days.

Only 1 month's supply may be given at a time and no refills can be obtained without a written prescription. Effects become evident within 30 minutes for most children and last 3-4 hours for the regular Ritalin. Ritalin also comes in a slow release form (Ritalin SR). The SR usually lasts 6-8 hours. The SR should not be chewed because all the medication could be released at one time. Studies are somewhat confusing about its efficacy. Most studies suggest that the SR is a little less effective than an equivalent dose of the regular Ritalin. Its advantages are that most children can get by without taking a second dose at school and they tend to have fewer emotional ups and downs than when taking the regular Ritalin. (For side effects, see "Side Effects of Stimulant Medication".) The medicine should not be used in psychotic children or in children who are taking MAO inhibitors for depression. There is a generic form that is significantly cheaper than the brand name. About 20% of children taking the generic Ritalin report that it is less effective than the brand name medication.

- Tablets 5mg, 10mg, 20mg.
- Time released (Ritalin SR) 20mg. Lasts 6-8 hours.

Adderall

Adderall is a mixture of four salts of a single-entity amphetamine and is now being used as often as Ritalin. It lasts 6-8 hours and has the advantage of having multiple-sized tablets available that are scored for ease of adjusting the dose. It is also inexpensive. It has the same potential side-effects as Ritalin. It has the same potential side-effects as Ritalin. Many states have laws requiring a special prescription that must be filled within 7 days. Only 1 month's supply may be given at one time and no refills can be obtained without a written prescription. Effects become evident within 30 minutes and last 6-8 hours. The medicine should not be used in psychotic children or in children who are taking MAO inhibitors for depression. The usual starting dose for children over age 6 is 5mg once or twice a day. Reports suggest that once-a-day dosing for school is possible by increasing the morning dose. The average dose is between 10-20 mg per day. This medication has the same addictive potential as Dexedrine.

- Scored Tablets 5mg, 10mg, 20mg & 30mg

Dexedrine

Dexedrine (dextroamphetamine sulfate) is the third most commonly used drug for ADD children. It has the same potential side-effects as Ritalin. Serum levels cannot be measured. Many states have laws requiring a special prescription that must be filled within 7 days. Only 1 month's supply may be given at one time and no refills can be obtained without a written prescription. Effects become evident within 30 minutes and last 4-5 hours. The medicine should not be used in psychotic children or in children who are taking MAO inhibitors for depression. The dosage is usually about one-half the Ritalin dose. Cost is generally cheaper than Ritalin. It has a higher potential to be abused than Ritalin.

- Tablets 5mg
- Time released Dexedrine spansules 5mg, 10mg, 15mg. Lasts 6-8 hours.

Dextrostat

Dextrostat (dextroamphetamine sulfate) is the same medication as Dexedrine but is cheaper and comes in tablets that are scored so that one-half and one-forth tablets can easily be given. It has the same potential side-effects as Ritalin. Serum levels cannot be measured. Many states have laws requiring a special prescription that must be filled within 7 days. Only 1 month's supply may be given at one time and no refills can be obtained without a written prescription. Effects become evident within 30 minutes and last 4-5 hours. The medicine should not be used in psychotic children or in children who are taking MAO inhibitors for depression. The dosage is usually about one-half the Ritalin dose. Cost is cheaper than Ritalin or Dexedrine. It has a higher potential to be abused than Ritalin.

- Tablets 5mg and 10mg

Cylert (See FDA warning)

Cylert (pemoline) is another available stimulant medication. This is a medicine that has been particularly effective for some adolescents. It has the advantage of being effective for 24 hours and is given once a day. The disadvantage is that it takes several weeks to determine if it is going to be effective. Most physicians feel that it has not been as beneficial as Ritalin or Dexedrine in the management of ADD. This medication also requires that blood tests be done periodically to monitor liver and blood toxicities. **The FDA has required the manufacturer to place a warning on this medication of potential liver damage. In the last twenty years there have been 13 patients who have experienced liver failure and death while on this medication.** There is only a slight chance of this occurring (there have been more than 60 million prescriptions written for this medication). **However, the FDA recommends that this drug only be used when others have failed and the person is in need of stimulant medication.** They recommend that liver studies be done on a regular basis but are not certain if these would predict liver problems. There is little potential for abuse. Dosage varies but usually is between 37.5mg - 122.5mg/day

- Tablets 37.5 chewable
- Capsules 17.5mg, 37.5mg, 75mg capsules

Medications – Tricyclic Antidepressants

Tofranil

Tofranil (imipramine) is effective in treating depressed children who have trouble with concentration. This medication is not as effective in treating attention and hyperactivity in the general ADD population as stimulants and requires monitoring for liver, blood and heart toxicities. The dose should be less than 2.5mg/kg in children. Effects might not be noted for 1-3 weeks. It is also used in the treatment of enuresis (bed-wetting).

- Tablets 10mg, 25mg, 50mg

Norpramin

Norpramin (desipramine Hydrochloride) has been found to have positive benefits for depression and seems to help attention problems also. Dosages have not been established but 50-100mg are being used in children with positive effects. Liver, blood, and cardiac toxicities need to be monitored. Several deaths have been reported in children on this medication. Effects are not apparent for 1-3 wks. Lower dosages produce the same blood levels when used in conjunction with stimulant medications.

- Tablets 10mg, 25mg, 50mg, 75mg, 100mg, 150mg

Medication – Selective Serotonin Reuptake Inhibitors (SSRI) Antidepressants

Prozac

Prozac (fluoxetine hydrochloride) has been found to be very effective in helping adults with depression. Studies are being done in adolescents to determine its effectiveness for treating depression in this age group. Several uncontrolled studies in children and adolescents suggest Prozac may be helpful in oppositional-defiant and conduct disorders. It has been shown to help adults with obsessive-compulsive disorders. Common side-effects include: headache, nervousness, insomnia, stomachache, nausea, constipation, and dry mouth. In a few cases it might aggravate suicidal ideation. Most of the side-effects can be prevented by starting with a low dose and gradually increasing. Adult dosage is 20mg - 80mg/day.

Pulvules 10mg and 20mg

Liquid 20mg/5cc

Paxil

Paxil (paroxetine hydrochloride) has benefits and side-effects similar to Prozac. Adult dosage is 20mg - 30mg/day.

- Tablets 20mg & 30mg

Zoloft

Zoloft (sertraline hydrochloride) has benefits and side-effects similar to Prozac. Adult dosage is 50mg - 200mg/day.

- Tablets 50mg & 100mg

Celexa

Celexa (citalopram HBr) Has benefits and side-effects similar to Prozac. Adult dosage is 20mg – 40mg /day.

- Tablets 20gmg & 40mg

Other Medications

***(These medications are not necessarily approved for the indications listed below by the FDA but they are being used by clinicians in the ways outlined below. Make sure your physician reviews the most recent indications and side-effects before starting them.)

***Clonidine

Clonidine is used to control high blood pressure in adults. Clonidine has been found to decrease activity levels in some adults.. It is one of the medicines of choice for children who have Tourette's Syndrome and attention problems because it slows down tics and decreases hyperactivity. However, it is less effective than the stimulant medications for most ADD children. Clonidine seems to help hyperactivity more than attention in ADD children. It also helps children who are easily over stimulated and have explosive behavior. It has the advantage of helping some children to sleep better. Clonidine should be started slowly and gradually increased so the child can get used to its sedative effect. Dosage is usually 2-3 times per day. There are transdermal patches that can be effective for up to a week but they are expensive and frequently cause skin irritation.

There have been some recent reports about cardiac arrhythmias when this medication has been used with stimulant medication. The combination of stimulants and Clonidine has been very beneficial for certain children with tics and attention problems. If used with stimulant medication, cardiovascular effects must be monitored closely. The medication should be stopped and the physician called if the child complains of chest pain, becomes pale or sweaty.

- Tablets 0.1mg
- Transdermal Patches

Tenex

Tenex (guanfacine hydrochloride) is an alpha 2 adrenergic agonist that has been used to lower blood pressure and is related to clonidine. It reportedly causes less sedation than clonidine. Once a day dosage is usually effective. It has the same indications as clonidine. Common side-effects include tiredness, dry mouth, dizziness and constipation. These side-effects are usually mild and disappear with time.

- Tablets 1mg, 2mg

Welbutrin

Welbutrin (bupropion hydrochloride) is an antidepressant not related to other types of antidepressants. It has been found to be effective in some ADD children helping both hyperactivity and attention. A major concern with its use is that seizures occur in 4 out of 1000 patients on this medication. Seizures increase with dosages above 300mg/day for adults. Other possible side-effects include agitation and insomnia, confusion, altered appetite, and allergic reactions. This medication should be used only in children who are not responding to more conventional treatments for ADD because of its risk of precipitating seizures.

- Tablets 75mg, 100mg

Anticonvulsants – Seizure Medication

Over the years physicians have tried treating ADD symptoms with anticonvulsants. Except in the case of petite mal seizures (staring spells lasting 3-7 seconds with a very specific brain wave pattern) these medications are not effective in helping the child's ADD problems. Many children have been placed on anticonvulsants when they have a slightly abnormal EEG (brain wave test). If the child has no obvious seizure activity, anticonvulsant therapy should not be used. Some of the anticonvulsants have been shown to slow learning in children and cause other potential problems. The anticonvulsants Tegretol and Depakane have been found to be beneficial in treating violent and aggressive behaviors in some children.

13

Controversial and Alternative Therapies

There are no quick fixes for children with handicapping conditions. It is only natural for parents to look for a quick cure. Many different therapies have been tried and no one therapy has proven successful by itself. We have discussed the proven therapies throughout this book. Medication is the closest thing to a quick cure, but it is far from perfect and is not without risk. There have been many other therapies proposed by well-meaning people; however, none of them have stood the test of time and none of them have been shown to be of benefit to ADD children in controlled studies.

Surveys now show that forty percent of patients have used some form of alternative medicine in the last year to treat their ailments. The major problem is that there is little scientific research on this type of treatment. There are only a few medical schools offering training to physicians in alternative medicine. However, the National Institute of Health is now funding the National Center for Complementary and Alternative Medicine (NCCAM). This agency is funding research on alternative treatments. Hopefully, within a few years we will be able to sort out fact (efficacious treatment) from fiction (snake oil).

Beware of the Following:

- Claims that a therapy cures all types of problems: ADD problems, behavioral problems, sleep problems, etc. There is no one therapy that works well in all areas.

- Therapies that use testimonials with no controlled scientific studies to prove a benefit.

- Therapies that claim to be natural. The word "natural" tends to be a marketing ploy and a way of avoiding FDA (Federal Drug Administration) requirements for proof of efficacy. Question therapies that are expensive and require a lot of money up front.

- Therapies that require you to use their product only.

Diets

As noted before, we believe ADD symptoms are caused by deficiencies of neurochemicals in the brain. It is felt that medications work by changing the concentration of these neurochemicals. If this theory is correct, then diet might affect the ADD child because food is the basic substrate for these neurochemicals. There are many therapies that have attempted to relate ADD symptoms to food groups or lack of foods. While these therapies are attractive because they do not use medication, they have not been shown to be effective for the majority of ADD children.

The Feingold diet is the most well known diet that has been used with ADD children. The theory is that certain foods cause children to become hyperactive (e.g. many parents have noticed that sugar is associated with hyperactivity). If these foods could be eliminated from the diet, then the hyperactivity would subside. While this is an attractive theory, controlled studies show that only 5% of ADD children respond favorably to the diet. Most of the studies suggest that medication is more effective than diet even in those children who respond to the diet.

Parents should not hesitate to try the diet, but if it is not effective for their child they should not feel guilty that they have not followed the diet closely. Obviously, most Americans have poor nutrition and all children could benefit from a more wholesome diet void of junk foods. There are no significant side-effects in trying the Feingold diet. The only detriment is the cost of buying foods devoid of preservatives, artificial coloring, and sugar. Parents find it hard to keep older children on the diet because of school lunches and visits to friends' homes.

Hypoglycemic Diets

Some people have suggested that low blood sugar is the cause of ADD symptoms. Certainly, children who are diabetics and have a low blood sugar have problems concentrating. No studies on ADD children have demonstrated problems with blood sugars. Therefore, diets designed to prevent hypoglycemia (low blood sugar) make little or no sense as a treatment for ADD.

Megavitamin and Orthomolecular Mineral

Most of these types of therapies were developed for adults and it is not known what dose of vitamins and minerals might be toxic to children. Mineral and vitamin therapy cannot be recommended at this time until more controlled studies have been done to determine potential benefits versus potential side-effects.

Hair Analysis

Many of those people advocating vitamin and mineral therapy support their therapies by evaluating hair. They use research that was done many years ago on prisoners showing that their hair analysis was different from a control group. This research had nothing to do with ADD children or adults but the proponents use it as a reason to add vitamins and minerals to the child's diet. Many of these programs require you to buy their vitamin and mineral supplements.

Yeast Infections (Monilial Infections)

A few people are blaming yeast infections for all sorts of problems that have no readily identifiable etiology. These include arthritis, chronic fatigue syndrome, behavioral problems, ADD, etc. It is true that the incidence of yeast infections has increased – probably because of the overuse of antibiotics. Any chronic infection can cause fatigue and behavioral changes. There is no evidence at this time that yeast infections have anything to do with ADD.

EEG Biofeedback

The newest fad treatment for ADD problems is electroencephalograph (EEG) biofeedback. This therapy is done by psychologists that hook the child up to an EEG machine (a machine that measures brain electrical activity by placing electrodes on the child's scalp). The machine evaluates which type of brain wave is the most prominent. The child is then asked to focus on a computer screen until the type of brain waves that are associated with paying attention are produced. The proponents of the system claim that they can cure ADD by using the system for 3-6 months. The cost of this therapy ranges from $3,000 to $6,000 dollars.

Most people would agree that practicing concentration would help the child improve the ability to focus attention. The EEG program would be a way to practice focusing attention.

Some Unanswered Questions

- Is there an easier and less costly way to practice focusing?
- Do the brain waves that the EEG is measuring have anything to do with attention? Many neurologists feel that they do not.
- What is the proof that this technique helps ADD children?

At this time, EEG biofeedback remains an interesting but expensive treatment. It cannot be recommended as a proven therapy until more scientific research is done.

Conclusion

Each of the above mentioned treatments is based somewhat on a scientific thesis. The question is whether that thesis has anything to do with what the proponents say it does. Probably there are subsets of ADD children who have benefited from the above listed interventions. However, none of the therapies has been proven to help the majority of patients and most are very costly.

Hint:

- If the alternative treatment sounds too good to be true, it probably is.
- Don't spend a lot of money on unproven therapies.
- Let the doctor know what vitamins, minerals and herbs are being taken. Some of these things can interact with prescribed medications.

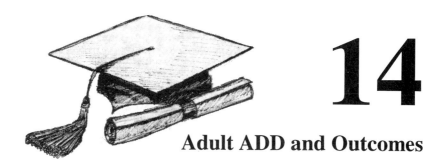

14

Adult ADD and Outcomes

Mr. Robertson brought his daughter in to be evaluated for school failure. The most striking feature that she presented with was an inability to concentrate and focus attention. She was eventually diagnosed as ADD without hyperactivity. Her treatment program included recommendations for the classroom and home to help her focus attention. This seemed to help some but she was still having a significant problem with getting work done. Tutoring was added to her program and she was started on Ritalin. This combined approach helped her begin to succeed. She went from failing grades to B work within two months. As the father learned more about his daughter's problems, he began to tell his story.

Mr. Robertson did not do well in school. He was called a bright child by his teachers, but they felt he was not motivated. In high school, he couldn't sit still in the classroom, he had trouble listening to the teacher's directions, and he never finished his homework. His teachers thought that he was lazy and unmotivated; however, his fellow students liked him because he was the best car mechanic in town.

Mr. Robertson quit school in the eleventh grade and went to work as a car mechanic. He couldn't stand to work in an enclosed garage, because he couldn't move around enough. He now is a very successful mechanic for the state highway department – he fixes the machines at job sites and he is still recognized as the best mechanic around.

He says he still has trouble sitting still and concentrating on any written material. Did he have ADD when he was a child? Does he still have ADD? These are difficult questions to answer.

Problems with Evaluating Adult ADD

The history is one of the most important parts in trying to evaluate whether a person has ADD. Many experts feel that ADD adults are usually not the best of historians. If they are not reliable, can information be obtained from parents and loved ones? For children we can ask the child's teacher to fill out a questionnaire; most adults would not want their employer to fill out an ADD questionnaire.

Several adult ADD programs have developed forms to help circumvent the problems noted above. The adult and a parent if possible are asked to fill out questionnaires. The programs also use structured interviews with the patient and if possible with a relative or spouse to help determine the diagnosis.

These programs are just starting to collect information on adult ADD patients. Many professionals didn't recognize ADD as a problem for adults until the early 1990's. Consequently, we do not have good information about treatment regimens or outcomes.

There are adults that have restlessness, difficulty concentrating, excitability, impulsivity, and irritability. These adults are called ADD-residual type if they have a childhood history compatible with ADD. There has been little research done on these adults. It wasn't long ago that everyone thought that children outgrow their ADD. We now know that most ADD children outgrow or control their hyperactivity but at least 30% still have the residual problems related to inattention, poor concentration, impulsivity, etc.

What can be done for these adults? The answers are not clear. Some authors have shown a benefit from stimulant medication while others have shown no benefit. What combinations of therapy might be helpful? Are there subgroups of adult ADD that are helped by specific therapies?

Each person who has had a handicap as a child is left with scars of that handicap. Sometimes the scars of the handicap are more important than the handicap itself. It would be important for the adult with ADD to find a professional who has knowledge about Attention Deficit Disorder.

In interviewing innumerable parents who fit the criteria as ADD-residual, it is my impression that the ones who are the most successful are ones who decided that their handicap (whatever it is called) was not going to keep them from succeeding in life. These adults have become successful by working hard.

What Do We Know?

At least a third of all children with ADD have significant problems in adult life related to their handicap. Many of these young adults still benefit from stimulant medication as they progress into adulthood. Once again adults are impacted both by their wiring and by their environment. Those adults who find their niche with a job that keeps their attention and interest do well in the game called life. Those who can't find their niche have a much more difficult time.

ADD Adults Wish They Had Had:

- Adequate remedial education in their school years.
- Tutoring in areas where they had deficits.
- Cognitive therapy to help them learn to use strategies to circumvent their weak areas.
- Individual psychotherapy to help them deal with the multiple frustrations that they encounter in life.

Treatment

Treatment should be directed towards helping the adult learn about the handicap. The adult should be taught compensatory strategies. Medication should be considered if the adult is having significant social, behavioral or work-related problems. It is beyond the scope of this book to go into specific therapies and protocols for helping adults with ADD. There are many books being written about adults with ADD. One of the best is *Driven to Distraction* by Edward M. Hallowell M.D.

Outcomes

We do have some decent information on young ADD adults. While this information might be skewed, because the initial diagnosis of ADD was made ten to fifteen years ago (when only more severe cases were diagnosed and multidisciplinary therapy was not used), it is still the best information that we have.

- ADD adults have had more academic, family, social, and personal problems than non-ADD adults.
- They are more likely to experiment with drugs.
- They are more likely to have automobile accidents.
- They have more job changes.
- They have more divorces.
- They are more likely to have run-ins with the law.

The above problems are a result of the core ADD problems of inability to focus attention, hyperactivity, and impulsive behavior. These characteristics tend to cause academic, social, and behavioral failures resulting in loss of self-esteem. The loss of self-esteem in turn leads to more failure.

Several studies have shown that ADD children who are mean are especially at risk for developing antisocial behaviors and have increased risk for run-ins with the law. If a child purposefully hurts other children or animals, they should be referred to a psychologist to work on these behaviors.

Good News

The good news is that over 70% of ADD children are successful adults. They learn to use their energy and creativity in positive ways.

Positive Factors Influencing Outcome

- Family
- Adolescents' I.Q.
- Length of drug therapy is not a factor

There are many factors that can influence the ADD child's outcome. The most important factor is the child's family. The family (especially the parents) can make all the difference in the world. The child will generally be more successful if the family can devote time and energy to the child. As mentioned before, the ADD child stresses even the most patient of parents. The parents must help the child psychologically, socially, behaviorally, and educationally. This is not a small task. It can be frustrating for the most patient of parents. However, if the parents can see this difficult task through, they will be rewarded with a child who will be successful.

ADD children who are naturally bright tend to be more successful than those of average intelligence. Bright children don't have to pay as close attention as others do. If the ADD child's creativity can be used and promoted, the child will tend to be more successful.

The use of stimulant medication has not been associated with negative outcomes. On the contrary, the judicious use of medication in combination with other therapies seems to give the child the best chance for a positive outcome. Some studies have shown that ADD children treated with stimulants had fewer car accidents, saw their childhood as being more positive, were less prone to steal, had better social skills, and had better self-esteem than untreated ADD children.

Conclusion

ADD is a handicap that can cause children to experience failure and frustration. This in turn can lead to social, behavioral, and academic problems. There is no one easy solution! The parents must set high expectations but not unattainable goals. They must make allowances so that the child can be successful without allowing the handicap to be used as an excuse. Successful parents focus on positives, help the child make good choices and value education.

Selected References

A.D.D. WareHouse (Catalog of books and supplies for ADD)
300 Northwest 70th Avenue, Suite 102
Plantation, Florida 33317   (800) 233-9273
http://www.addwarehouse.com

CH A.D.D. (Support Group for Parents and Adults with ADD)
8181 Professional Place, Suite 201
Landover, MD 20785
(800)-233-4050   (301)-306-7070 FAX (301)-306-7090
http://www.chadd.com

American Psychiatric Association: *Diagnostic and Statistical Manual of Mental Disorders*, Fourth Edition. (DSM-IV). Washington, DC: American Psychiatric Association, 1994.

Duke, Marshall P., Nowicki, Stephen Jr. and Martin, Elisabeth A. (1996). *Teaching Your Child the Language of Social Success.* Atlanta: Peachtree Publishers.

Hallowell, Edward M., and Ratey, John J. (1994). *Driven to Distraction.* New York: Pantheon Books.

Hallowell, Edward M., and Ratey, John J. (1994). *Answers to Distraction.* New York: Pantheon Books.

Johnson, Spencer, M.D., (1998). *Who Moved My Cheese?.* New York: G.P. Putnam's Sons.

Kotulak, Ronald (1993, April 11-15). Unraveling hidden mysteries of the brain. *Chicago Tribune.*

Nowicki, Stephen, and Duke, Marshall P. (1996). *Helping the Child Who Doesn't Fit In.* Atlanta: Peachtree Publishers.

Phelan, Thomas (1994). *Surviving Your Adolescents.* To order call 1-800-442-4453.

Phelan, Thomas (1993). *1-2-3 Magic.* To order call 1-800-442-4453.

Whitley, Michael D. (1996). *Bright Minds Poor Grades.* Response Publishing Inc.